Copyright 2013 Harvard Business School Publishing

All rights reserved

Printed in the United States of America

10 9 8 7 6 5 4 3

No part of this publication may be reproduced, stored in or
introduced into a retrieval system, or transmitted, in any
form, or by any means (electronic, mechanical, photocopying,
recording, or otherwise), without the prior permission of
the publisher. Requests for permission should be directed to
permissions@hbsp.harvard.edu, or mailed to Permissions,
Harvard Business School Publishing, 60 Harvard Way, Boston,
Massachusetts 02163.

Library of Congress Cataloging-in-Publication Data

O'Connell, Andrew (Business writer)
 Stats and curiosities : from Harvard business review / written
and edited by Andrew O'Connell.
 pages cm
 ISBN 978-1-4221-9631-1 (alk. paper)
1. Success in business. 2. Selling–Psychological aspects.
I. Harvard business review. II. Title.
 HF5386.O248 2013
 650.1–dc23

 2013018855

The paper used in this publication meets the requirements
of the American National Standard for Permanence of Paper
for Publications and Documents in Libraries and Archives
Z39.48-1992.

stats

& curiosities

from
HARVARD BUSINESS REVIEW

written and edited by
ANDREW O'CONNELL

HARVARD BUSINESS REVIEW PRESS

BOSTON, MASSACHUSETTS

contents

introduction:
curiouser and curiouser

Someone studied *that*? Someone actually studied the relationship between company performance and the width of the CEO's face? That was my first response on reading an academic paper on leaders' facial dimensions. I often react that way when I encounter the more unusual studies in out-of-the-way journals. Someone really estimated my likelihood of dying in the week after I get a bonus? Someone actually studied the effect of organic food on my moral judgments? Someone calculated the percentage of Prius drivers who ignore pedestrians in crosswalks?

But in four years of writing the Daily Stat, *Harvard Business Review*'s online digest of reports from the front lines of research in business, economics, and psychology, I've come to appreciate the breadth and depth of the topics

being examined in laboratories and field studies around the globe.

For one thing, many of the findings published in the Daily Stat and compiled in this book turn out to be surprisingly useful: Background noise and a glimpse of green can make you more creative. Two-person teams are quicker than four-person teams.

Other stats are entertainingly odd: A taste of sugar gives people greater self-control. Disgust makes people more receptive to the new.

Most important, the data tells us a story about who we are: Single male CEOs take bigger financial risks in order to appear more attractive. Better-educated workers are less satisfied with their lives. High-status individuals are more likely to believe that people are smiling at them. There are two main messages in all this: Even in a high-tech age, we integrate our most human foibles and vulnerabilities into our work. And Prius drivers should *watch where they're going.*

—Andrew O'Connell

mysteries
of the
human
brain

We start at the source, with an exploration of the nature of the mind. The brain, of course, is responsible for our greatest achievements and oddest behaviors, and, for better or worse, we bring it with us to the office every day. There we let it loose to do all the things it has been doing since we evolved as humans, such as seeking advantage over our coworkers and misinterpreting the world. On a product-safety note, Margaret Neale of Stanford and Scott Wiltermuth of the University of Southern California point out in this chapter that reading too much useless information makes you 46% less likely to think clearly, so as you peruse these stats, please read responsibly.

high status gives people delusions of approval

Research subjects who had been primed to think of themselves as having elevated status reported seeing **19% more** smiles on the faces of people who had judged their work than subjects who considered themselves to have low status, say Nathan C. Pettit of NYU and Niro Sivanathan of London Business School. That's because a person's status colors his or her perceptions of others' approval. Thus it seems evident that of all the rewards for achievement—recognition, income, promotion—the most valuable is the high-status mind-set, the researchers say.

2

powerful people think they're taller

People who were asked to summon up memories of being powerful judged themselves to be an average of **6 inches taller**, in comparison with a pole, than people who were asked to remember being powerless, say Michelle M. Duguid of Washington University and Jack A. Goncalo of Cornell University. Moreover, being physically elevated makes a person both feel powerful and seem powerful to others, the researchers say.

men with shaved heads are perceived as bigger and stronger

Shaven-headed men seen in photographs were perceived as **an inch taller** and **13% stronger** than men with full heads of hair, according to an experiment reported by the *Wall Street Journal*. Albert Mannes of The Wharton School says he conducted his study after noticing that he was treated with greater deference after shaving off his hair. His research shows that men with shaved heads are seen as more dominant than men with full hair, and men with thinning hair are seen as the least powerful of all.

4

consumers are repelled by worn-out money and want to spend it

People who were given worn-out $20 bills spent **82% more** of the money than consumers who were given four crisp $5 bills, reversing the expected "denomination effect," which typically leads people to spend less from larger-denomination bills, say Fabrizio Di Muro of the University of Winnipeg and Theodore J. Noseworthy of the University of Guelph, both in Canada. People tend to be disgusted by worn bills and want to get rid of them because of presumed contamination from other people, the researchers found.

5

pain makes you indulge afterward

Research participants who had been induced to plunge their hands into ice water subsequently took **73% more** pieces of candy from a bowl than those who hadn't experienced pain, says a team led by Brock Bastian of the University of Queensland in Australia. Because people perceive pain as a form of punishment, they respond by feeling entitled to indulge themselves, particularly if they believe the pain was unfairly inflicted, the researchers say.

6

a task looks lighter when help is promised

People who were asked to guess the weight of a box of potatoes gave an estimate that was **10% less** if they were told they'd get help lifting it, according to a team led by Adam Doerrfeld of Rutgers University. When participants were told they'd have to lift the box solo, they correctly guessed it weighed **10.5 pounds**, on average. When they were informed that another person would help them, they guessed **9.4 pounds**. Our perceptions are shaped not only by what we can do by ourselves but by what we believe we can do with others' help, the researchers say.

a glimpse of green makes people more creative

Research participants who got a two-second glimpse of a green rectangle completed a subsequent task of imagining various ways to use a tin can with about **20% more** creativity than those who had seen a white rectangle, says a team led by Stephanie Lichtenfeld of the University of Munich in Germany. It's unclear why green, as opposed to red, blue, or gray, would stimulate creativity, though the researchers point out that green has strong associations with growth in many cultures.

8

red makes you push for a better deal . . .

When an online negotiable-price vacation package was presented against a blue background, research subjects made a "best offer" of **$712**, on average, but they went only as high as **$684** when the background was red. Rajesh Bagchi of Virginia Tech and Amar Cheema of the University of Virginia say red induces aggression, so it heightened participants' competitiveness with the seller and increased their determination to get a good deal. Red has the opposite effect in auctions, where greater aggression makes people willing to pay more in order to best other bidders, the researchers say.

$684
AVERAGE "BEST OFFER" ON A RED BACKGROUND

$712
AVERAGE "BEST OFFER" ON A BLUE BACKGROUND

100 200 300 400 500 600 700 800 900

. . . and makes male diners tip more

Male diners give bigger and more frequent tips to waitresses wearing red T-shirts than to those wearing black, white, blue, green, or yellow, according to Nicolas Guéguen and Céline Jacob of the Université de Bretagne-Sud in France. There's no such effect from female customers, however, a finding that aligns with research suggesting that red increases women's attractiveness to men. The study was conducted in France, where tips are generally included in the bill and additional tipping is considered optional. **40.7%** of male diners in the study provided additional tips to waitresses, compared with **33.1%** of females.

10

single ceos, wishing to seem attractive, take bigger risks

Companies run by unmarried CEOs appear to invest more aggressively and take greater risks—their investment level is **10% higher**, on average, and their stock-return volatility is **3% greater** than other firms', say Nikolai L. Roussanov of The Wharton School and Pavel G. Savor of the University of Pennsylvania. The numbers are consistent with evidence that single men take on greater risk than their married peers in hopes of being more attractive to potential mates, the researchers say.

do you think of time as proceeding left to right or right to left?

Research participants viewed a weight-loss ad more favorably (scoring it **4.64** on a 7-point scale) when a "before" picture was placed on the left and an "after" picture was placed on the right, in comparison with when the picture locations were reversed (**3.39** on the same scale), say doctoral candidate Boyoun (Grace) Chae and JoAndrea Hoegg of the University of British Columbia. That's because the participants, who grew up using left-to-right languages such as English, conceptualize time as proceeding from left to right. The effect is reversed among people from cultures that read right to left, even if those cultures read numbers from left to right, the researchers say.

12

anti-atheist bias is based on distrust of nonbelievers

In a series of psychological experiments conducted in Vancouver, Canada, participants revealed that they considered atheists to be less trustworthy than a number of groups often considered to be outliers, including Muslims, gay men, and feminists, and **only as trustworthy** as rapists, according to a team led by Will M. Gervais of the University of British Columbia. The lack of trust in atheists may reflect people's assumption that individuals tend to behave more ethically if they believe they are being monitored by a higher power, the researchers suggest.

prospective students like elite colleges better on cloudy days

A **1-standard-deviation increase** in cloud cover on the day of a prospective student's visit to an elite university was associated with a **9-percentage-point increase** in the probability that the student would enroll, says Uri Simonsohn of The Wharton School. In a study of 1,284 prospective students, Simonsohn found evidence that cloudy weather makes academic activities more appealing and increases the desirability of attending an academically challenging institution.

14

when you feel cold, you like romance movies better

Because being physically cold makes people crave psychological warmth, it also increases their preference for romance movies, according to a series of studies by Jiewen Hong of Hong Kong University of Science and Technology and Yacheng Sun of the University of Colorado. For example, undergraduates were willing to pay about **$1.60** (US) more to see a romance movie when the ambient temperature was about **13 degrees** (Fahrenheit) colder. The effect didn't apply to action movies, thrillers, or comedies.

reading irrelevant information hurts your ability to think

Research participants who had read useless information about future negotiation partners were **46% less likely** to identify important issues in the negotiation than people who had been told nothing, suggesting that irrelevant information hampers clear thinking, say Scott S. Wiltermuth of the University of Southern California and Margaret A. Neale of Stanford. Moreover, statements such as "This person prefers a certain amount of change and variety and becomes dissatisfied when hemmed in by restrictions and limitations" tended to be rated as advantageous, indicating that the participants were unable to perceive the uselessness of the information they were given, the researchers say.

16

thoughts about time's monetary value inhibit pleasure

Research subjects who had been asked to calculate their recent hourly wages were less happy (scoring an average of **63** on a scale of 100) while listening to "The Flower Duet" from the opera *Lakme*, by Leo Delibes, than those who hadn't been prompted to think about their wages (**70** on the same scale), say Sanford E. DeVoe and Julian House of the University of Toronto's Rotman School of Management. Thinking about time in terms of money impairs people's ability to derive happiness from pleasurable experiences, the researchers say.

the taste of real sugar improves self-control

People who rinsed their mouths with lemonade containing sugar were **9% faster** in identifying the font colors of on-screen words, a task that has been shown to demand self-control, than people who rinsed with artificially sweetened lemonade, says a team led by Matthew A. Sanders of the University of Georgia. Rinsing the mouth with glucose may improve self-control by activating brain areas associated with reward, the researchers say.

18

younger siblings take more risks, even in baseball

In a study comparing siblings who play major league baseball, researchers found that younger brothers are **10.6 times** more likely to try to steal bases—and **3.2 times** more likely to be successful at it. Frank J. Sulloway of UC Berkeley and Richard L. Zweigenhaft of Guilford College analyzed the performance of 700 brothers who were major leaguers in an effort to test a hypothesis from evolutionary theory that younger siblings are more likely than older siblings to participate in high-risk activities.

disgust makes people more receptive to the new

51% of people who viewed disgusting images from the film *Trainspotting* were willing to trade a closed box of office supplies for a new one, compared with just **32%** of people who weren't exposed to the repellent images, say Seunghee Han of Chung-Ang University in South Korea and Jennifer Lerner and Richard Zeckhauser of Harvard University. Incidental feelings of disgust thus appear to disrupt the deeply held "status quo bias" that leads people to favor what they already have over something new, the researchers say.

20

a fishy smell
makes people
more suspicious

People who had been exposed to a fishy smell in a hallway were willing to invest **24% less** money with another person, suggesting that fishy smells induce suspicion and undermine cooperation, at least among English speakers, say Spike W. S. Lee of the University of Toronto and Norbert Schwarz of the University of Michigan. The blending of metaphor and reality goes both ways, the researchers say: Being suspicious also makes people more likely to literally smell something fishy.

bad
behavior,
good
behavior

Lying, stealing, cheating, and booing the opposing pitcher: This is the dark side of the Organization Man (and Woman). If the findings in this chapter hit too close to home and burden your conscience, bear in mind the message that's implicit in the research of Claudia Townsend of the University of Miami and Wendy Liu of UC San Diego: Planning to improve your behavior can backfire. Maybe it's better just to accept yourself and stay the way you are.

criminals are more likely to target people seen as deviant

Car wash attendants who cleaned the interiors of automobiles stole loose change **30%** of the time, but the rate **doubled** if the driver had left a beer can and a racy magazine in the car, say Ronald Burns, Patrick Kinkade, and Michael Bachmann of Texas Christian University. The experiment suggests that you're more likely to become a victim of petty crime if would-be criminals see you as more socially "deviant," the researchers say.

22

iphone thefts
skew crime stats
in new york

Thefts of Apple products such as iPhones significantly skew crime statistics in New York City, says the *New York Times*. Thefts of the company's products rose by **3,890** in 2012 over 2011; without that increase, overall crime in the city would have been **down** for the year. Thefts of non-Apple devices declined, officials said.

under-the-table is the way to get public contracts in china

More than **90%** of experts responding to a survey in China said that a company conducting under-the-table practices to influence decision makers would have a better chance of winning a public-project contract than a company that followed all the rules, say Xuguang Song of Beijing Normal University and Wenhao Cheng of Tsinghua University, both in China. The survey of academics in 36 cities also indicated that Shanghai is perceived to be the **most corrupt** city in China. On a more positive note, **more than half** of respondents said their cities had become less corrupt.

24

you're more selfish when you feel close to a selfish person

People who were encouraged to identify with a selfish individual became more selfish, keeping **11% more** cash when they were asked to divide money between themselves and another person, say Francesca Gino of Harvard Business School and Adam D. Galinsky of Northwestern University's Kellogg School. The reason for the effect: when people feel psychologically close to someone who behaves selfishly, they're more likely to consider the behavior to be less shameworthy and less unethical, the researchers found.

it helps to boo the opposing pitcher

Baseball pitchers threw **40% fewer** strikes when the crowd jeered than when it cheered, according to an experiment led by L. Kimberly Epting of Elon University. The research, which took place in a college setting, shows that the real value of fans' behavior during a game may be in their antagonism toward the opposing team, the authors say. Basketball players' free-throw accuracy, however, was the same whether the crowd was cheering or jeering.

26

decline of unions increases burglaries and theft

The decline in union membership in the United States from 1993 to 2006, and the consequent loss of well-paying blue-collar jobs, increased property crime by **15%**, according to an analysis by Robert Baumann and Bryan Engelhardt of the College of the Holy Cross. Moreover, each **1-percentage-point decrease** in unionization increases burglaries, larceny, arson, and auto theft by roughly **140 crimes** per 100,000 people. Well-paying jobs deter crime by increasing a criminal's potential cost of spending time in prison. The proportion of unionized workers declined from **23.5%** in 1973 to **12.4%** in 2008.

many financial pros feel pressure to compromise ethics

30% of financial services professionals say their compensation or bonus plans create pressure to compromise ethical standards or violate the law, according to a survey in the United States and UK conducted for the law firm Labaton Sucharow. **22%** of female respondents say they'd face retaliation if they reported wrongdoing in the workplace, compared with **12%** of male respondents.

28

male professionals with higher ethical standards earn less

Although companies have focused greater attention on the need for ethical practices over the past few decades, male business professionals who self-report high ethical character earn, on average, **3.4% less** than their peers who don't report having such standards, according to an analysis of data on thousands of students by Andrew Hussey of the University of Memphis. Moreover, men who reported that their MBA programs enhanced their ethical standards received **6.5% lower** wages than men who reported no such gain. For women, the situation is different: female professionals who self-report high ethical standards receive no pay penalty, and women who said that their schooling had raised their standards received a premium averaging **5.5%**.

richer executives are more likely to be indicted for insider trading

Executives who are indicted for insider trading tend to be **just as rich** as or **richer** than other top managers. In fact, the likelihood of being indicted on this charge increases with compensation and wealth, according to a study of 52 accused executives by Utpal Bhattacharya of Indiana University and Cassandra D. Marshall of the University of Richmond. The motive for the crime thus may have more to do with hubris or company culture than a desire for money. The benefit that Martha Stewart would have received from her alleged insider trading was just **0.007%** of her $650 million net worth in 2001, the authors say.

30

making plans to be good can cause you to act badly

Planning ahead is usually seen as beneficial for self-control. But in a study of people with low savings who got a US stimulus rebate in 2008, those who were instructed by researchers to plan their use of the money ended up spending about **38% more** of it on purchases as opposed to saving or investing, say Claudia Townsend of the University of Miami and Wendy Liu of UC San Diego. There was no such effect for people with high savings. That's because if you're already behind on a goal, planning to further the goal can be stressful and can undermine your self-control, the researchers suggest.

what happens to your smartphone after you lose it

72% of people who found "lost" smartphones in five cities tried to access photos, **57%** tried to open a file named "Saved Passwords," and **43%** tried to open an app named "Online Banking." Symantec's experiment involving 50 phones deliberately left in food courts, restrooms, and other locations also showed that just half of the finders tried to contact the owners, whose phone numbers and e-mail addresses were prominently shown in the phones' contact lists, according to Credit.com's report on the study.

32

high percentage of hybrid drivers ignore pedestrians in crosswalks

About **one-third** of drivers of Prius hybrids failed to yield to pedestrians in a series of experiments on crosswalks in the San Francisco Bay area, giving the brand one of the highest rankings for "unethical driving," say psychologist Paul Piff of the University of California, Berkeley, and a team of colleagues. Drivers of hybrids "who believe they're saving the Earth may feel entitled to behave unethically in other ways," says Piff, who is quoted on news.sciencemag.org.

people lie more in e-mails than face-to-face

When getting to know new people, about **70%** of people lie about things ranging from their feelings to their achievements, but the incidence of deception is higher over e-mail than in face-to-face meetings, say Mattitiyahu Zimbler and Robert S. Feldman of the University of Massachusetts. In a study of undergraduates' 15-minute conversations with same-sex individuals, those using e-mail had **5 times more** lies per word communicated than those speaking face-to-face. Lying appears to be more common when the communicator is psychologically and physically distant from the person receiving the message, the researchers say.

34

volunteerism drops as governments raise social spending

An increase in government spending on social benefits by **1 percentage point** of GDP decreases an individual's likelihood of volunteering for religious, sports, arts, or any other kind of organization by about **2 percentage points**, say Franz Hackl, Martin Halla, and Gerald J. Pruckner of the University of Linz in Austria. Another factor that diminishes volunteerism is the population's confidence in its elected officials. Among the countries with the smallest proportions of adults doing unpaid work are Hungary, Japan, and Spain, at **16%**; at the other end of the spectrum are Sweden, the Slovak Republic, and the United States, with volunteer rates of **56%**, **54%**, and **50%**, respectively.

why kenyan bus passengers yell at their drivers

Inexpensive messages urging Kenyan minibus passengers to heckle and criticize their drivers for being reckless caused a **60% reduction** in insurance claims involving injury or death, say James Habyarimana and William Jack of Georgetown University. Stickers carrying messages aimed at passengers such as "Don't just sit there as he drives dangerously! Stand up. Speak up. Now!" and showing graphic illustrations of severed feet and legs were placed inside the buses. Drivers were given incentives to leave the stickers in place.

36

moral sentiments seem to arise from a single molecule

An infusion of the neurohormone oxytocin into research participants' noses increased their generosity **80%** in an experimental game, suggesting that this molecule is responsible for humans' moral sentiments, says Paul J. Zak of Claremont Graduate University. A previous study showed that an oxytocin infusion can more than double the number of subjects who trusted a stranger with all their money.

to your health

These days, we're inundated with health advice from sources as diverse as newspapers, doctors' bulletin boards, and fortune cookies. But only here will you learn that forcing yourself to smile by gripping chopsticks in your teeth might reduce your stress level, as is suggested by Tara L. Kraft and Sarah D. Pressman of the University of Kansas. What this behavior might do to your coworkers' stress levels is a subject for further research.

the effect of college drinking is like having a bad teacher

Drinking alcohol depresses college students' academic performance by roughly the same amount as having a bad professor for an entire semester, according to a team led by Scott E. Carrell of the University of California, Davis. In a study of students at the US Air Force Academy, where underage drinking is tightly controlled, the researchers found that performance dropped by **one-tenth of a standard deviation** after students turned 21 and were allowed to drink, an effect that lasted **8 months** and, surprisingly, was most pronounced for the best students.

38

thoughts of organic food reduce your desire to be helpful

People who viewed images of food labeled "organic" made harsher moral judgments about others' behavior and volunteered **6 minutes less** of their time to help someone out, compared with people who viewed nonorganic foods, says Kendall J. Eskine of Loyola University New Orleans. The findings suggest that morality and "ethical" foods occupy the same conceptual "space" in people's minds, with the result that exposure to organic foods helps people affirm their moral identities and reduces their desire to be altruistic, Eskine says.

a simple pain reliever reduces hurt feelings

Daily doses of acetaminophen taken by undergraduates over the course of 3 weeks alleviated hurt feelings from social rejection, according to Nathan DeWall of the University of Kentucky. Humans' social-pain system functions much like the physical-pain system; nevertheless, more research is needed on whether any analgesic is an effective means of treating social pain, DeWall says.

LEVEL OF HURT FEELINGS

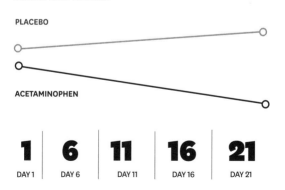

PLACEBO

ACETAMINOPHEN

1	**6**	**11**	**16**	**21**
DAY 1	DAY 6	DAY 11	DAY 16	DAY 21

40

south korea's mass pardons of traffic offenders led to more accidents

Since 1995, 4 presidents of South Korea have issued mass pardons to drivers who had lost their licenses because of drunk driving, vehicular homicide, and other violations. About **24.6 million people**, more than **10%** of the country's population, have benefited from these populist gestures, but the pardons increased traffic accidents by an average of **4.3%** in the subsequent years, says a team led by Youngsun Kwon of Korea Advanced Institute of Science and Technology. Arbitrary and irrelevant pardons can be considered an abuse of clemency power, the researchers suggest.

dad's layoff diminishes baby's birth weight

The birth weights of babies born after their fathers lose their jobs are **4.7% lower, or about 5 ounces less**, than those of employed dads' babies, according to Jason M. Lindo of the University of Oregon. In a study of American fertility data from 1968 to 1997, Lindo says the effect may be due to factors such as the reduced food expenditures that result from lower family income and the stress experienced by moms who work more actively after their husbands are laid off.

42

social participation provides the same happiness boost as a gigantic raise

Regular participation in clubs and other social activities increases happiness to the same degree as **doubling** one's income or obtaining a college degree, according to Harvard's Robert D. Putnam, as reported by Chris M. Herbst of Arizona State University. Evidence indicates that social connectedness has a powerful influence not only on happiness but also on self-reported health, Herbst says.

forcing yourself to smile can reduce stress

The heart rates of people who were recovering from the stress of tracing a star with their non-dominant hands were **7% slower** if they gripped a pair of chopsticks in their teeth in such a way as to force themselves to smile, say Tara L. Kraft and Sarah D. Pressman of the University of Kansas. While the researchers acknowledge that the generalizability of their findings is questionable given the artificiality of the setting, they say the study shows there are physiological and psychological benefits from maintaining a positive facial expression during stress.

44

the presence of happy people appears to raise suicide risk

Countries and US states with higher happiness levels tend to have higher suicide rates, says a team of researchers led by Mary C. Daly of the Federal Reserve Bank of San Francisco. For example, Utah is ranked **number 1** in life satisfaction but has the **9th-highest** suicide rate, whereas New York, ranked **45th** in satisfaction, has the **lowest** suicide rate in the United States. Unhappy people may become suicidally distressed by others' contentment, the researchers suggest.

the unemployed exercise more, but get less exercise

Working people expend more physical energy than the unemployed, even though they spend an average of **27% fewer** minutes exercising each day because of the demands of their jobs, according to Gregory J. Colman of Pace University and Dhaval M. Dave of Bentley University. In a study of thousands of US workers, the researchers found that after employees are laid off, their total daily physical exertion declines between **21% and 24%**, despite increased levels of recreational exercise.

46

one way to get consumers to eat less: offer smaller portions

Up to **33%** of people ordering at a fast-food Chinese-style restaurant in the United States accepted an explicit offer to be served smaller portions of starchy side dishes, according to a team led by Janet Schwartz of Tulane University. Those who accepted the smaller portions didn't compensate by ordering higher-calorie entrées. Activating consumers' self-control in this way is more effective in reducing diners' intake than mandated calorie labeling, the researchers say.

choosing extra large makes you seem high-status

People who were observed choosing large-size coffees, pizzas, and smoothies were rated by others as having higher status—an average of **4.98** on a 1-to-7 scale—than people who chose small sizes (**3.03**), according to an experiment led by David DuBois of HEC Paris. The research shows, moreover, that people who feel powerless tend to choose larger options than people who feel powerful, regardless of the item's price. The findings have implications for the high rate of obesity in developed countries, particularly among people with low socioeconomic status, the researchers say.

48

will falling rates of driving lead to lower obesity?

A study of car and light-truck use in the United States between 1985 and 2007 shows that each increase in daily vehicle travel by **1 mile per licensed driver** was associated with a **2.16% increase** in the adult obesity rate 6 years later, says a team led by Sheldon H. Jacobson of the University of Illinois. The number of miles per driver had been rising until 2004, when it leveled off. In 2007, miles driven began **falling**, but it's unclear whether that drop will lead to lower obesity rates, the researchers say.

caffeine content of espressos varies wildly

In a sampling of espresso servings from 20 coffee shops near the University of Glasgow in Scotland, researchers found a huge range of caffeine content. The 52-milliliter serving from Patisserie Francoise had **6 times** the caffeine of the 27-milliliter serving from Starbucks, reflecting variations in blends, roasting processes, and barista technique. The risk that you'll unwittingly get a megadose of caffeine from your next espresso is unlikely to be limited to Glasgow, the researchers say.

the working
world

Here we begin to shift from the personal to the professional, from the individual to the corporate sphere. The workplace, as you'll see in this section, is an endlessly fruitful area of research, partly because people spend such a large proportion of their lives there. Though maybe not quite as much as they *say* they do: As John P. Robinson of the University of Maryland discovered, employees do love to tell tales about their work hours.

being sleepy makes you more inclined to surf the web at work

For every hour of interrupted sleep the night before, research participants engaged in **8.4 minutes more** cyberloafing—checking personal e-mails or visiting unrelated websites—during a 42-minute task, says a team led by David T. Wagner of Singapore Management University. The effect of lost sleep on cyberloafing at work is supported by data showing that on the Monday after the switch to Daylight Savings Time, Google users search for **3.1%** to **6.4% more** entertainment-related websites in comparison with other Mondays.

51

some managers juggle well, some don't

A **third** of the executive teams surveyed by Vangelis Souitaris of Cass Business School in London and B. M. Marcello Maestro of the investment firm Bravemarket were highly "polychronic," meaning they displayed a preference for interruptions. About **half as many** were highly "monochronic," preferring to focus deeply. Polychronic teams' faster decision making boosted their companies' performance.

HIGHLY POLYCHRONIC

"We multitask all the time, not simply because we can—but because we want to."

AVERAGE 50%

HIGHLY MONOCHRONIC

"It doesn't matter if anyone thinks one project is less revenue-generating than another. Once we're on it, our absolute priority lies in finishing what we've started."

34%

16%

"This team prides itself on being able to oversee several ongoing projects at the same time quite easily...We enjoy the variety, that constant switching, the challenge of needing to concentrate harder."

"Hopping from one project to another? Is that really wise? I mean, there is no time to really think things through, right? I believe it would only ruin our concentration and disrupt our thought process."

Quotes are from the researchers' study of executives of nearly 200 tech firms on the London Stock Exchange.

52

going to work seems to take longer than coming home

The journey from home to an office or any other destination feels longer than the return trip, according to a series of studies by Priya Raghubir, Vicki G. Morwitz, and Amitav Chakravarti of New York University. In one experiment with 127 undergraduates, for example, participants estimated that it took them an average of about **22 minutes** to go from home to the classroom, but just **17 minutes** to get back. The reason, the researchers suggest, may be that people mentally define the destination "home" as a relatively large area and unfamiliar destinations as relatively small.

a longer commute leads to more absenteeism

Workers with a 50-kilometer one-way commute can be expected to miss **15% more** days from work, on average, than their colleagues who commute 10 kilometers, according to a study of workers in Germany by Jos N. van Ommeren and Eva Gutiérrez-i-Puigarnau of VU University in Amsterdam. Commuting distance is usually assumed to affect only employees, not businesses, but the study shows that it also has a strong impact on absenteeism.

telecommuters are more productive on creative tasks, less on dull ones

A telecommuting experiment involving university students shows that working remotely reduces productivity by **6%** to **10%** if the task involves typing randomly generated characters but boosts productivity **11%** to **20%** for the job of imagining unusual uses for a tin can, says E. Glenn Dutcher of the University of Innsbruck in Austria. So if a task is tedious, an employer should make sure it's done in the office, but when it comes to creative work, a manager might do best to allow employees to work remotely, Dutcher says.

you get the biggest bang from an mba if you've never held a job

For people who go to business school with no prior work experience, the average return on an MBA program is about **20%**. But that **drops** for people who have held jobs before getting their MBAs, sinking to as low as **2.2%** for people who have **19 years'** prior experience, according to a study of thousands of students by Andrew Hussey of the University of Memphis. The MBA is primarily a "signaling" device that is most effective when a candidate has a skimpy CV. Hussey estimates that **89.6%** of the return to the average MBA program comes from the message it sends to prospective employers, rather than from knowledge gains that would make students more productive.

56

why you lose
motivation halfway
through a task

Research participants who were assigned to proof-read nine essays found an average of **0.122 typos per second** at first, then just **0.092 per second** at the halfway point of the experiment, then **0.124** near the end, revealing a U-shaped, "stuck in the middle" pattern of motivation over the course of a task, says a team led by Andrea Bonezzi of Northwestern University's Kellogg School. At the beginning of a chore, people tend to be motivated by their progress in relation to the starting point; at the end, they're spurred on by their proximity to the end point. In the middle, their motivation flags because their attention shifts from the starting point to the end point, the research suggests.

don't believe people who say they work 60 hours a week

People overstate the number of weekly hours they "usually" work by **5% to 10%,** with those on the higher end being more likely to overestimate, according to a study led by John P. Robinson of the University of Maryland. By examining US workers' time diaries, the researchers found that people who say they usually work **55 to 64 hours per week** are off by an average of about **10 hours;** people who say they work **65 to 74 hours** are overstating by about **20 hours.** Respondents may inflate their estimates because of a desire to appear industrious, the researchers suggest.

google discovers the optimal lunch-line waiting time

Researchers for Google's HR department have found that the wait for lunch in the cafeteria should be about **3 or 4 minutes**—no more, no less. That's just long enough for employees to meet new people but still short enough not to be a time-waster, according to *Slate*. And lunch tables should be long, so workers who don't know each other are forced to sit together and chat.

ceos get very little time to think and work alone

In a typical 55-hour workweek, CEOs spend an average of just **6 hours** working alone, according to a study by researchers from the London School of Economics and Harvard Business School. The *Wall Street Journal* reports that **18** of the CEOs' weekly hours were spent in meetings, **5** were occupied by business meals, and **4** were spent in phone calls and conference calls, with much of the rest devoted to miscellaneous activities ranging from travel to personal appointments.

60

flattering the boss can set him up for a fall

A **1-standard-deviation increase** in the amount of flattery and ingratiating agreement that CEOs receive raises their likelihood of being fired by **64%**, say Sun Hyun Park and James D. Westphal of the University of Michigan and Ithai Stern of Northwestern University. Flattery inflates leaders' opinions of their abilities and prevents them from making changes in the face of poor corporate performance. Over a 12-month period, colleagues and close subordinates admitted making an average of **3.64** statements to CEOs complimenting them in ways that slightly exaggerated the leaders' insight on strategic issues, the researchers say.

it's not work that keeps people from interacting

Would people interact more if they didn't have to work so many hours? Apparently not, suggest Henry Saffer of the US National Bureau of Economic Research and Karine Lamiraud of ESSEC Business School in France. After France reduced the workweek from **39** to **35 hours** in 1998, workers spent more time reading, listening to music, exercising, being with their children, cleaning, shopping, washing, cooking, and relaxing—but didn't spend time on additional social interaction, the researchers found.

would you recommend your job to your children?

67% of people in agriculture and ranching say they'd recommend their jobs to their offspring, by far the highest percentage of any industry, according to an online survey of nearly 3,000 respondents by Salary.com. The next highest are professional services (**44%**), IT (**43%**), health care (**42%**), energy and utilities (**41%**), engineering and design (**36%**), education (**36%**), and arts and media (**36%**). The workers *least* likely to recommend their jobs to their kids are in hospitality and tourism (**25%**), finance and banking (**24%**), and retail (**18%**). Overall, just **36%** say they'd recommend their line of work to the next generation.

more workers are giving up their personal work space

60% of 950 companies surveyed by the International Facility Management Association say they now have unassigned work spaces in their offices, and about half say the number of employees using unassigned desks has risen over the past two years, according to the *Wall Street Journal.* In an effort to boost creativity and save on space, American Express designates some **20%** of the 5,000 people at its New York headquarters as "club" employees, meaning that they're on-site less than full-time and work at unassigned desks.

the cure for workplace misery: a manager who cares about employee development

60% of US government employees studied by Gallup say they don't clearly know what's expected of them at work. That's because a lot of government workers are stuck with lousy managers, according to Jim Clifton, Gallup's CEO. If an organization hires managers who care about employees' development, workplace misery magically disappears, Clifton says.

gender gaps

All it takes is a glance at academic journals to notice that there's a tsunami of research on gender in the workplace. That's probably a good thing. Ideally, these studies demolish stereotypes and allow us to see beyond the sex gap so that we can better appreciate people's humanity. Sort of like the girl-power conversion that happens to male CEOs when they have firstborn daughters, as you'll see.

more men than women are ashamed of their wages

26% of men but just **17%** of women say their friends would feel badly for them if they knew how much money they really earned, according to a survey of 5,000 people by the FIT, a website of the recruiting-technology company Bullhorn. Not only are women less ashamed of their salaries, they also report working longer days and working more on vacation than men, and they're less likely to take a sick day under false pretenses, the survey says.

men are more economically impulsive when they outnumber women

When unmarried men in an experiment perceived that they outnumbered unmarried women, they raised their intended borrowing by an average of **$372** per year and cut their intended yearly savings by an average of **$756**, according to a team led by Vladas Griskevicius of the University of Minnesota. An overabundance of males appears to intensify competition for mates, leading men toward greater economic impulsivity. The findings suggest that sex ratios may have far-reaching consequences for many economic decisions and, potentially, whole economies, the researchers say.

being agreeable hurts earnings, especially for men

Young men who are agreeable—who are more cooperative and place greater value on relationships—earn **20% less** than their peers, on average, according to a study led by Timothy A. Judge of the University of Notre Dame. Put another way, men who are **1 standard deviation less** agreeable than the mean earn **18% more** than men who are 1 standard deviation more agreeable than the mean. For women, agreeableness has a similarly negative effect on earnings, but it is much less severe, according to the study of thousands of Americans.

68

moms talk about numbers more to boys than to girls

In interactions with toddlers, American mothers use number terms **twice as often** when they speak to boys as when they speak to girls, according to a team led by Alicia Chang of the University of Delaware. The study of 32 two-year-olds also found that moms use explicit quantifications (for example, "four crayons") **2.7 times more** frequently when speaking to boys than to girls. Although gender-stereotypical use of language may be inadvertent, past research shows it can affect children's interests and their perceptions of their own numerical competence, the researchers say.

ex–east germans retain strong egalitarian views on gender roles

People from the former East Germany are **28 percentage points more** likely than former West Germans to believe that it's good for children to have working mothers, and **22 percentage points more** likely to disagree that wives should stay home, say Stefan Bauernschuster and Helmut Rainer of the University of Munich. The findings show that decades after reunification, socialism-inspired attitudes about sex roles strongly persist among former East Germans and that the gap in egalitarian beliefs between East and West has only widened, the researchers say.

salaries rise after ceo's wife has firstborn daughter

The wages of employees—especially women—rise after a male CEO's wife delivers a daughter who is the couple's first child, according to research conducted in Denmark and reported in the *Wall Street Journal*. Female employees' salaries grow an average of **1.1%** after the birth, compared with a **0.6% gain** for males. Past research suggests that men sometimes care more about other people's well-being after having daughters. When male CEOs have sons, workers' salaries **decline** by an average of **0.4%**.

women's competitiveness drops when fertility is low

Women who use contraceptive pills are **50% less competitive** during the 21 days of the month when they take the drug, which contains the sex hormone progesterone, according to Thomas Buser of the University of Amsterdam. Moreover, in an experiment involving compensation schemes for a problem-solving task, women were **10.5 percentage points less** likely to opt for a competitive scheme if they were at the point in their monthly cycles when fertility was low because progesterone levels were high. The findings are consistent with evolutionary theories positing that competitiveness is less useful for women during the infertile phase of the ovulation cycle. Some researchers have said that aversion to competition may help explain the low number of women in top corporate positions.

why a female scientist in a pink dress is no hero to girls

Adolescent girls' plans for taking college math **drop** if they're shown feminine-looking women excelling in technological fields. After 11- to 13-year-old girls heard about women who were successful in science and wore dark-colored clothing, their expectations of taking math averaged **5.57** on a 1-to-7 scale, say Diana E. Betz and Denise Sekaquaptewa of the University of Michigan. But when girls learned about science-achieving women who wore makeup and pink clothes, their expectations of taking math fell to **4.04**. Feminine-looking scientists may seem a rare breed to gender-stereotyping adolescents, and past research suggests that unattainable role models are more threatening than inspiring.

black is the attire of choice for female senior execs

51% of female senior executives typically wear black to work, compared with just **18%** of their male colleagues. But the preponderance of males gives the C-suite an overall bluish hue: with men and women counted together, **36%** of senior executives typically wear navy blue, **26%** favor black, **8%** prefer brown, and **8%** prefer gray, according to a CareerBuilder survey of more than 550 hiring managers in leadership positions. **63%** of senior executives typically wear business casual; only **14%** wear suits.

74

more older women are marrying younger men

The proportion of male-female partnerships in which the woman is at least five years older than the man increased sharply in the UK and the United States in the 1980s and 1990s: Having remained at about **3%** for decades, it rose to **8.3%** in 2000 and is likely much higher now, say Melvyn G. Coles and Marco Francesconi of the University of Essex in the UK. Today's wider career choices give women the opportunity to increase their desirability through financial success, an option that once was limited to males, the researchers say.

a stranger's touch while shopping is a turnoff

Shoppers in a UK store were negatively affected by a stranger's seemingly accidental touch on the shoulder, particularly if the toucher was male, says Brett A. S. Martin of Queensland University of Technology in Australia. The touched shoppers evaluated brands more negatively, spent less time in the store, and reported that they were willing to pay about **40% less** for a particular item than untouched shoppers. Prior research shows that customers respond favorably to intentional touch, such as from store employees.

76

after divorce, dads can help their kids by moving away

A child whose parents are divorced and whose father is highly educated will later have **12% higher** earnings if the dad moves away to a distant location, according to a study led by Ariel Kalil of the University of Chicago of data on nearly 16,000 children in Norway. The father's decision to move away also increases the likelihood that the child will stay in school longer and makes the child **5.4 percentage points more** likely to be working at age 27. The effects, which apply only to college-educated dads, may be due to these men's greater involvement with their children after divorce and the consequent disruptions, such as overnight visits and parental conflict, in the children's lives, the researchers say.

when women began voting, budget deficits shrank

Enfranchisement of women in Switzerland led to reductions in local budget deficits of between **139 and 148 Swiss francs per capita**, say Signe Krogstrup and Sébastien Wälti of the Swiss National Bank. Women's gradual enfranchisement in the country's 26 cantons from 1959 through 1990 enabled the researchers to examine the effect on local government spending. They speculate that the reasons for the declining deficits have to do with women's altruism, patience, and prudence toward risk.

78

commuting stresses women more than men

The stress of commuting is **4 times greater** for women with preschool-age kids than for men with children of that age, according to a team led by Jennifer Roberts of the University of Sheffield in the UK. In general, women tend to be more distressed than men by time wasted getting to and from work, all the more so if errands such as food shopping are added to the women's trips. Women who are unaffected by the daily commute fall into three categories: single with no children, able to work flexible hours, and reliant on partners who are responsible for the bulk of child care.

why his merit raise is bigger than hers

When research participants were asked to imagine that their organization emphasized merit and that they needed to allocate $1,000 in bonuses, they tended to favor men, giving them **$46 more** per person, on average, than they awarded to comparably performing women, say Stephen Benard of Indiana University and Emilio J. Castilla of MIT. The bias was exhibited by male and female managers alike. Managers in organizations that champion the idea of meritocracy may relax their vigilance about fairness and allow their biases greater sway, the researchers say.

MEAN BONUS AWARDED, IN $

400 — **399** | **401**

375 — | | | **374**

350 —

0 —

MALE EMPLOYEES | **FEMALE EMPLOYEES** | **MALE EMPLOYEES** | **FEMALE EMPLOYEES**

420

NOT AN EXPLICIT MERITOCRACY | **EXPLICIT MERITOCRACY**

When people in an experiment were told that their company was a meritocracy, they gave bigger bonuses to men.

women get a
bigger wage boost
from exercise

Frequent exercise boosts wages, but the increase is much more pronounced for women than for men, according to Vasilios D. Kosteas of Cleveland State University. Women who exercise frequently earn **11.9% more**, on average, than women who don't—a premium that's approximately equal to the effect of **1.8 additional years'** schooling. For men, the wage benefit of frequent exercise is **6.7%**, equivalent to about **1.3 years more** school, Kosteas says. The findings are consistent with the hypothesis that beauty and fitness matter more for women's wages than for men's.

why women pay more for mortgages: they don't shop

Women's mortgage rates in the United States are an average of **40 basis points higher** than men's—a significant burden, considering that women's median household income is less than **half** that of men, says a team of researchers led by Ping Cheng of Florida Atlantic University. The reason for the mortgage disparity: men tend to search for the lowest rates, whereas women seem to prefer dealing with lenders recommended by other people, the researchers found.

america the statistical

t's a land renowned for its wealth and power, but research shows that America is also a land of inequality and dissatisfaction, a place where divisions of many kinds, from racial to political, can have far-reaching consequences. It's also a place where people seem to have an awful lot of trouble remembering to redeem their gift cards.

firms with politically conservative bosses pay more tax

US companies with Republican-leaning top executives pay an average of **$12 million**, or about **2.2%**, more tax annually than companies led by Democrats, according to research led by Dane Christensen of the University of Arizona. A conservative mind-set in the C-suite may discourage companies from pursuing risky or questionable strategies for avoiding taxes and thus may result in higher tax expenditures, the researchers suggest. Republican-leaning top executives outnumber their Democrat-leaning peers by about **2 to 1**.

US-born are half as likely to start businesses as immigrants

Native-born Americans are **half** as likely to start new businesses as immigrants, and among US natives, whites are the only major demographic group to show a **decline** in the share of all new entrepreneurs from 1996–2011, according to the Ewing Marion Kauffman Foundation. The Latino share of new entrepreneurs during that period rose from a little more than **10%** to **22.9%**, reflecting increased entrepreneurship among the group as well as a growing share of the US population. The Asian share of new entrepreneurs also rose substantially, but remains modest at **5.3%**. The African American share increased slightly.

among blacks, parental layoffs are more likely to keep kids out of college

The negative effect of parental job loss on children's likelihood of going to college is almost **3 times stronger** for blacks than for whites in the United States, say Ariel Kalil of the University of Chicago and Patrick Wightman of the University of Michigan. When blacks lose their jobs, they're more likely to face long-term unemployment, which may undermine family wealth and lead to parental depression, marital conflict, and behavioral problems among children, the researchers say. The findings underscore the economic fragility of America's black middle class.

whites have benefited more from pay-for-performance jobs

The rise of "pay for performance" has fueled earnings inequality in the United States by boosting wages at the high end of the spectrum, but a close look shows that it has had a much bigger effect on whites than blacks, say John S. Heywood of the University of Wisconsin and Daniel Parent of HEC Montreal. Whites earn **31% more** when they take pay-for-performance jobs, but the differential for blacks is only **12%**. The reasons may have to do with high-wage blacks' apparent preference for government jobs, which are less reliant on bonuses, the researchers suggest.

GE's high-deductible health plans hurt its own businesses

Use of expensive medical imaging such as MRIs in the United States has **dropped** by as much as **one-quarter** in the past couple of years, partly because many health plans now have high deductibles, which prompt patients to weigh the benefits of imaging against the high cost, according to the *Wall Street Journal*. Among the big companies to offer such health plans is General Electric, which as a maker of MRI machines has been hurt by the reduced demand for imaging.

number of stay-at-home dads rises dramatically

The number of American men who have completely left the workforce to raise children has more than **doubled** over the past decade to **176,000**, according to a *New York Times* report on census data. Some **half a million** other dads serve as primary caretakers for their families while maintaining freelance or part-time jobs. More men now feel it's socially acceptable to be stay-at-home dads, even if secure jobs are available to them, the *Times* says.

gays boost home prices in liberal areas, depress prices in conservative areas

The addition of **1** same-sex couple for every **1,000** households is associated with a **1% increase** in home prices in US neighborhoods that are socially liberal, but a **1% drop** in neighborhoods that are extremely conservative, say David Christafore of Konkuk University in South Korea and Susane Leguizamon of Tulane University. Their study of more than 20,000 real estate transactions in Ohio in 2000 supports previous findings that migration of same-sex couples to an area increases home values, in part because these residents tend to develop or enhance cultural amenities. But the new research suggests that in socially conservative areas, housing prices reflect prejudice against gays.

americans carry big money in unused gift cards

The typical American home holds an average of **$300** in unredeemed gift cards, according to an estimate reported by Rocky B. Cummings and Joseph Carr in the *Journal of State Taxation*. These cards are often misplaced, accidentally thrown out, or only partially redeemed. Between 2005 and 2011, **$41 billion** in gift cards went unused, the authors say. But retailers don't always benefit: many states require issuers to report unclaimed balances as abandoned property after a prescribed period of time.

2000 may have been the worst year to retire

Because of poor investment returns, Americans who retired in 2000 with nest-egg assets divided 60/40 (stocks/bonds), withdrawing 5% annually and paying a 1% fee, had an average of just **54%** of their wealth remaining 10 years later, the **worst** 10-year performance of any retiree cohort (until that date) since 1926, says Wade D. Pfau of the National Graduate Institute for Policy Studies in Tokyo. Poor returns at the beginning of retirement can lead to early wealth depletion that becomes difficult to overcome. Pfau says even the old **4%** rule-of-thumb annual withdrawal rate from retirement assets may be overly optimistic if stock and bond returns are low.

americans' satisfaction waned as connections withered

Between 1985 and 2005, the number of Americans who said they definitely felt satisfied with the way their lives were going dropped by about **30%**, and the ranks of the most dissatisfied rose by nearly **50%**, according to a study involving thousands of people by Chris M. Herbst of Arizona State University. The reasons appear to be related to Americans' declining attachments to friends and family, lower participation in social and civic activities, and diminished trust in political institutions, Herbst says. The only good news: the rate of decline in satisfaction appears to have slowed during that two-decade period.

top US execs earn 17 times what their counterparts make in china

The average combined salary and bonus for top corporate executives in the United States is about **17 times higher** than the comparable figure for China, say Martin J. Conyon of Lancaster University and The Wharton School and Lerong He of SUNY Brockport. If equity-based pay such as stock options is included, the multiple jumps to **42 times**. One possible explanation: there is a more active market for superstar senior executives in the United States, the authors say.

american teens feel meh about cars

The proportion of American teenagers with drivers' licenses fell from **64.4%** in 1998 to **46.3%** in 2008 as young people soured on the idea of owning and driving cars, according to the *New York Times*. When 3,000 millennials were asked to name their preferred brands, the top 10 included no automobiles. Carmakers are realizing they need to take radical steps to adjust to young people's changing tastes.

single adults in united states may soon outnumber those in marriages

The number of single people in America is growing at **more than twice** the rate of those who are wed, and if that trend continues, single adults will soon account for a larger share of the US population than married couples for the first time on record, according to CNN.

firms provide more stock options in areas with fewer protestants

A **1-standard-deviation increase** in the ratio of Catholics to Protestants in the surrounding region translates into a **19.31% increase** in the value of stock options provided by local companies to their nonexecutive employees, according to a team led by Alok Kumar of the University of Miami. That's because stock options have characteristics in common with gambling, which Protestants have traditionally shunned as sinful, the researchers suggest. Catholics, by contrast, tend to hold a tolerant view of gambling; some Catholic organizations even raise funds through bingo tournaments.

contradiction alert: declines in home equity shrink charitable donations . . .

Households increase their gifts to charity by nearly **1%** for every **10% increase** in home equity. That's about **10 times** the effect of increases in other types of wealth such as stocks and bonds, say Chau Do and Irina Paley of the US Treasury. The finding may be ominous for charities: a long-lasting **20% decline** in US home equity would mean a **$52-per-homeowner** decrease in donations, or about **$3.8 billion less** for charities nationwide, the researchers say.

. . . but in hard times, people spend more on charity (and cigarettes)

In a recession that shrinks GDP by 2%, consumers increase their charitable expenses by **32%**—about the same proportion by which they reduce their expenditures on jewelry and watches (**35%**), according to Wagner A. Kamakura of Duke University and Rex Yuxing Du of the University of Houston, who studied purchases by more than 66,000 US households over 2 decades. Consumers also increase their tobacco expenditures by **16%**. People are more likely to start smoking (and resume smoking after quitting) in recessions than in good times, the researchers say.

when walmart arrives, other supermarkets shape up

Local supermarkets reduce stock-outs by an average of **10%** and boost product variety after a Walmart supercenter opens nearby, according to a study by David A. Matsa of Northwestern University's Kellogg School. Despite persistent grass-roots opposition to Walmart's spread into US communities, the supercenters spur existing supermarkets to make significant improvements, especially in poor areas, Matsa says. Competition from Walmart has been linked to bankruptcies of at least **25** supermarket chains.

skilled players earn much bigger returns from poker

Poker players who were identified as being highly skilled achieved an average return on investment of **30.5%** during the 2010 World Series of Poker, whereas other players averaged a **minus-15.6%** ROI, according to research by Steven D. Levitt of the University of Chicago and Thomas J. Miles of the University of Chicago Law School. Their analysis of the 720 players in the tournament supports the notion that poker is a game of skill, not purely of chance, a key factor that US courts have struggled with in trying to determine the legality of the multibillion-dollar online poker industry.

economic
realities

Widening our focus now to the whole world, we explore cause and effect on a macro level. These are weighty issues: What happens to worker satisfaction when education levels rise? What are the consequences when youth populations dip? Do companies fare better after they separate the CEO and chairman roles? And why do people become stingy when they take an economics course?

raising corporate taxes is good, not bad, for jobs

An increase of **10 percentage points** in the corporate tax rate is associated with a drop of **2.1 percentage points** in the unemployment rate, according to a study by Horst Feldmann of the University of Bath in the UK of data on 19 industrial countries. Although raising corporate taxes has been shown to reduce economic growth, it also unexpectedly prompts companies to substitute labor for capital and spurs unions to reduce their wage demands in order to avoid job losses, Feldmann says.

materialism underlies singapore's low birth rate

People living in Singapore are more materialistic and less satisfied with life than their American counterparts and thus have a lower desire for children, says a team led by Norman P. Li of Singapore Management University. It is apparently at least in part for this reason that the fertility rate in Singapore, at **1.09** births per woman's lifetime, is about **half** the US fertility rate of **2.05**, the researchers say. Fertility rates in Hong Kong, Japan, Singapore, South Korea, and Taiwan have dropped below levels required to sustain the countries' populations.

newspapers make politicians behave better

A study in Norway by Christian Bruns and Oliver Himmler of the University of Goettingen in Germany shows that a better-informed electorate induces politicians to behave better. Each **1-standard-deviation increase** in a newspaper's circulation or coverage of local news leads to governmental efficiency gains of between US**$368,000 and $460,000** annually for a municipality of an average population of 10,600.

most individual investors do far worse than the s&p 500

The S&P 500 index substantially outperforms individual stock-market players and even most professional investors, according to Todd Feldman of San Francisco State University. Over a recent 20-year period, the average US individual stock investor got an annual return of just **1.9%**, while the S&P 500 returned **8.4%**, and over a recent 5-year period, the S&P 500 outperformed **68.6%** of actively managed large-cap funds. Investors' most destructive mistake is basing long-term predictions on what is happening in the current environment, a behavior known as "anchoring," Feldman says.

airlines' profit amounts to revenue from 1 in 100 passengers

If a US airline collected $16,400 in fares and fees for a typical (hypothetical) domestic flight, just **$164** of that would become profit, according to an analysis by US Airways and Oliver Wyman for the *Wall Street Journal*. In other words, if there were 100 passengers, the total profit would be represented by just **1** traveler's fare and fees. Fuel costs would eat up the revenue from **29** passengers; salaries, **20**; ownership costs, **16**; government fees and taxes, **14**; maintenance, **11**; and "other" costs, **9**.

you're more likely to win if you trail at the half

Professional basketball teams that are behind by **1 point** at halftime win more often than teams that are ahead by **1 point**, according to an analysis of more than 18,000 NBA games by Jonah Berger of The Wharton School and Devin Pope of the University of Chicago. In many contexts, being slightly behind appears to increase motivation and effort, the researchers say (the exhibit on the next page shows the performance of typing-contest participants who were informed they were "slightly behind").

INCREASE IN NUMBER
OF KEYSTROKES PER
30 SECONDS

COMPETITIVE FEEDBACK BETWEEN ROUNDS

How participants in a typing contest responded, on
average, to feedback on how they were doing.

after 9/11, road deaths rose as americans avoided flying

In the aftermath of the September 11, 2001, terrorist attacks, fear of flying spurred Americans to drive more miles, and the additional miles led to increased traffic fatalities, say Wolfgang Gaissmaier and Gerd Gigerenzer of the Max Planck Institute for Human Development in Berlin, Germany. There were **1.11 additional** traffic fatalities per 1 million inhabitants, on average, in the United States during the post-September months of 2001; typically, fatalities decrease slightly during those months of the year, the researchers say.

lawsuit-protection insurance leads executives to make poor choices

Entrenched executives and directors who are insured against shareholder lawsuits tend to make worse M&A decisions, according to a team led by Chen Lin of Chinese University of Hong Kong. For example, their firms' average acquisition premiums (the percentage amounts they pay above the targets' stock price) are more than **twice** those paid by firms with uninsured officers. The findings suggest that the threat of litigation can lead to better investment choices, but only if corporate officials aren't shielded by liability insurance.

broadband boosts well-being as effectively as a robust economy

A **10-percentage-point increase** in broadband penetration produces the same lift in the population's subjective well-being as a **2.89% increase** in GDP per capita, say Georgios Kavetsos of Cass Business School and Pantelis Koutroumpis of Imperial College Business School, both in London. In fact, ownership of a range of high-tech devices, including phones, CD players, and computers, is associated with significantly higher levels of satisfaction, according to their study of 29 countries, most in Europe. The researchers found no such effect for ownership of TV sets, however.

companies' borrowing practices reflect their bosses'

Companies whose CEOs have borrowed 100% of the value of their homes have debt ratios that are **7.2 percentage points higher**, on average, than those of comparable firms led by CEOs with zero mortgage debt, says a team led by Henrik Cronqvist of Claremont McKenna College. In their study of chief executives of large US firms, the researchers found that, overall, bosses tend to push their companies' capital structures toward the debt levels they feel comfortable with in their personal lives. A strong board can reduce the value-destroying effect of CEOs' tendency to imprint their personal leverage preferences on the firm, the researchers say.

better-educated workers are less satisfied

Job satisfaction is lower among people who are more educated and who are single, and higher among public servants. Moreover, job satisfaction follows a U-shaped course over a lifetime, starting high before dipping and then rising again, says Santiago Budría of the University of Madeira. Workers with secondary and tertiary education are about **2 percentage points more** likely to be completely unsatisfied with their jobs and **2 to 4 percentage points less** likely to be fully satisfied, according to a study of nearly 5,000 workers in Spain.

some pay taxes because it feels good . . .

Why do people pay taxes so willingly, even when penalties for nonpayment are weak? Because they like the way it makes them feel, say Diego Lubian and Luca Zarri of the University of Verona in Italy. In a study of thousands of Italians, the researchers discovered that greater willingness to pay taxes is associated with greater levels of personal happiness, a finding that dovetails with research showing that cheating has psychological costs such as guilt and a diminished self-image. **79%** of those surveyed said they strongly felt that paying taxes is one of the duties of citizenship.

. . . yet aversion to taxes runs deep

The proportion of Americans who said they'd travel 30 minutes to save 8% on an item by getting it tax-free (that is, free of an 8% sales tax) was **29% bigger** than the proportion who said they'd travel the same distance to get an ordinary 9% discount, according to a series of experiments by Princeton doctoral student Abigail B. Sussman and Christopher Y. Olivola of the University of Warwick in the UK. And more than **4 times** as many Americans said they'd rather invest in a bond that offered a $120 annual tax-free return than a bond that offered $160 but required a $40 tax. The findings reveal an aversion to taxes that extends beyond monetary costs, the researchers say.

companies do worse if they split the ceo and chairman roles under pressure

Companies that bow to investor pressure and split the CEO and board-chair positions, rather than allowing the CEO to hold both jobs, tend to fare worse than comparable firms on a number of metrics, says a team led by Aiyesha Dey of the University of Minnesota. For example, companies that make this change under pressure are associated with returns on assets that are **1.8% lower** than companies that switched without pressure and **3.4% lower** than control firms, on average. The findings contradict the view that board-leadership structures are created to meet the self-serving needs of CEOs and that splitting the roles will lead to performance improvements, the authors say.

114

the pay cut is a good tool for managing bad ceos

Corporations are increasingly likely to use pay cuts to respond to poor CEO performance, and for good reason: In a study of 927 instances of 25% pay cuts from 1994 to 2005, a team led by Huasheng Gao of Nanyang Technological University in Singapore found that companies' median stock return goes from **minus 8%** in the pay cut year to **plus 10%** in the subsequent year, and return on assets improves as well. Corporations are twice as likely to impose sharp pay cuts as to dismiss poorly performing CEOs, the researchers say.

researchers easily prove false findings

Using legitimate statistical analyses, researchers were able to show in an experiment that participants were nearly **1.5 years younger** after listening to the Beatles' "When I'm Sixty-Four" than after listening to a song that comes with the Windows 7 operating system—an obviously ridiculous finding that demonstrates how easy it is for research to yield "false positives," say Joseph P. Simmons and Uri Simonsohn of The Wharton School and Leif D. Nelson of UC Berkeley. Too often, researchers aren't aware of the high likelihood of finding false evidence, and the pressure to publish leads scientists to convince themselves of the validity of their findings, the authors say.

when you sell your phone, you sell your data

Researchers who examined 49 secondhand mobile phones were able to extract an average of **227** pictures, e-mails, and other items per device, and they found that about half the phones contained sensitive personal items, including images of nudity, and one contained sensitive business information, according to a team led by William Glisson of the University of Glasgow. Using standard forensic tools on the phones, which were purchased on eBay and in a pawn shop, the researchers were able to recover deleted items from **31** of the phones.

catholics get higher returns on human capital

In Australia, Roman Catholic men earn **6.7% more** than men of other religions, according to a study of household data by Michael A. Kortt of Southern Cross University and Brian Dollery of the University of New England, both in Australia. Their findings are consistent with research showing that in the United States, Catholic men ages 26 to 34 benefit from an estimated wage premium of **7.1%**. The researchers speculate that a Catholic upbringing instills attitudes and work habits that employers value.

the pill made cohabitation part of the marriage-partner selection process

The birth-control pill didn't cause American women to forgo marriage in favor of cohabitation, but it did help make cohabitation a part of the mate-selection process, says Finn Christensen of Towson University. Access to the pill is associated with a **6.1-percentage-point increase** in the probability that women cohabited with their husbands before marriage. The pill became widely available to single women after the Supreme Court struck down a Massachusetts law in 1972.

cohabitation, then marriage, leads to greater wealth

People who cohabit with just one person and then marry that person go on to accumulate wealth at **double** the rate of people who marry without cohabiting, according to a study of US couples by Jonathan Vespa of The Ohio State University and Matthew A. Painter II of the University of Wyoming. About **one-third** of married people in the United States have cohabited, in most cases with just one person (relatively few people are serial cohabiters).

120

to drive creativity, add some conformity

Groups with a variety of cognitive types produce higher levels of innovation, say Ella Miron-Spektor, Miriam Erez, and Eitan Naveh of Technion-Israel Institute of Technology. In a study of 41 radical-innovation teams of a large defense contractor, the researchers found that the best recipe was: **20%** to **30%** creatives, up to **10%** detail-oriented members, and **10%** to **20%** conformists, who support the creatives, boost cooperation, and improve team confidence.

WHAT'S THE OPTIMAL BALANCE?

About 50% of people have a mix of thought patterns, but the rest fall into 1 of 3 distinct cognitive types. The best radical-innovation teams have a sprinkling of the 3.

CREATIVES are the source of radical-innovation ideas, but they're not always attentive to usefulness, may initiate conflict, and don't care much about rules, so teams too heavily weighted with them may have trouble with implementation. On the most innovative teams studied, creatives accounted for

20% to 30%

CONFORMISTS support the creatives, boosting cooperation and improving a team's confidence. On the most innovative teams studied, conformists accounted for

10% to 20%

DETAIL-ORIENTED PEOPLE may strengthen functions such as budgetary control, but they're skittish about taking risks. On the most innovative teams studied, detail-oriented people accounted for

up to 10%

121

economics courses make students less generous

College economics courses have the effect of making noneconomics majors less generous, at least toward nonprofits. Taking introductory microeconomics reduces a nonmajor's likelihood of donating to specific nonprofits by **2 percentage points**, and an intermediate course reduces the likelihood by **3.7** to **7.9 percentage points**, according to Yoram Bauman and Elaina Rose of the University of Washington. It's unclear whether this is the result of exposure to economics concepts, exposure to economics faculty and students, or some other cause, the researchers say.

alcoholism in russia hampers work and careers

7% to **8%** of Russia's people have been accused by police of unlawful acts stemming from alcohol abuse, and an estimated **3.4%** of the population are alcoholics, a rate **1.5** to **2 times higher** than for most of Europe, says Grigorii Grigorevich Zaigraev of the Russian Academy of Sciences. Moreover, of the 720,000 children living in orphanages, more than **600,000** are "social orphans" whose parents have been stripped of parental rights due to alcohol abuse. The spread of drunkenness seriously limits Russian people's ability to acquire professions needed to make a living, Zaigraev says.

couples argue 3 times per month about finances

Financial matters trigger an average of **3** arguments per month for married couples, an incidence that rises to **4** per month for those ages 45 to 54, according to a US survey conducted for the American Institute of CPAs by Harris Interactive. The most common source of contention is disagreement over what's a "want" and what's a "need." The next most common issues are unexpected expenses and insufficient savings.

dips in youth populations may trigger recessions

More than **70%** of major declines in the proportion of 15-to-24-year-olds in the population have been associated with declines in GDP growth, according to a study of worldwide data from 1960 through 2005 by Diane Macunovich of the University of Redlands in California. A boom in the population of young people seems to boost producers' expectations, and the passing of the bubble causes defaults and bankruptcies, which prompt foreign investors to withdraw funds and speculators to unload the local currency. This appears to have been the pattern in 4 financial crises since 1980, as well as in Japan's "lost decade," Macunovich says.

125

online chatter volume predicts stock prices

Researchers were able to do **7.9% better** than the S&P 500 stock index by (virtually) investing in brands that generate high volumes of online chatter. In studying 4 years' worth of product reviews of 15 brands, Seshadri Tirunillai of the University of Houston and Gerard J. Tellis of USC's Marshall School found that sheer volume of reviews and negative chatter have a strong predictive relationship with stock returns, with negative chatter predicting lower stock prices; positive chatter and 5-star ratings have no predictive value. The stock-return effects are rapid but not immediate: they follow bursts of user-generated comments by a few days, the researchers say.

wide-faced CEOs' companies perform better

Companies led by wide-faced male CEOs had industry-adjusted returns on assets that were up to **$16 million greater** than firms led by narrow-faced men, according to a study headed by Elaine M. Wong of the University of Wisconsin-Milwaukee. A higher width-to-height ratio in men's faces is linked to higher aggression, a greater sense of personal power, and more untrustworthiness in personal interactions, the researchers say.

the arc
of life

Here we look at the span of human experience from childhood through schooling and on to retirement. This section offers several valuable life lessons: Be mindful of what you put on Facebook, don't be fatalistic, and ask someone else to drive after you get your bonus check.

why parents feel broke

The total cost of raising a child to full independence in the Northeast United States, including food, clothing, health care, housing, transportation, entertainment, half of a typical college tuition, and lost parental wages, comes to **$1.8 million**, calculates journalist Nadia Taha. Concern that she might not be able to guarantee financial security for her family is a major factor in her decision not to have children, Taha writes in the *New York Times*.

children in big families get less, but achieve more

Each additional child in a family is associated with **higher** reading scores, even though additional births reduce parents' investments in their offspring. In a study by Marc Frenette of the Social Research and Demonstration Corporation in Canada, the number of computers per child in homes with 6 children was **64% lower** than in homes with 2 children, and parents in 6-child homes were **54% less likely** to have saved for college than parents in 2-child homes. Parents of large families may be more likely to be out of the workforce, and their presence in the home may boost children's abilities. Another possibility is that parental investments in children ultimately have **no effect**, Frenette says.

children are affected by parents' entrepreneurial attempts

Offspring between the ages of **18 and 21** are the most strongly affected by their parents' success or failure as entrepreneurs, according to Edward Mungai, dean of Strathmore Business School in Nairobi, Kenya, and S. Ramakrishna Velamuri of the China Europe International Business School in Shanghai. Young adults who witness a parent's entrepreneurial success are more likely to try self-employment themselves, but a parental failure witnessed at that time discourages entrepreneurism.

mom and dad's attitude about risk affects children's achievement

Children of risk-averse parents have lower test scores and are **1.34 percentage points less likely** to attend college than offspring of parents with more-tolerant attitudes toward risk, says a team led by Sarah Brown of the University of Sheffield in the UK. Aversion to risk may prevent parents from making inherently uncertain investments in their children's human capital; it's also possible that risk attitudes reflect cognitive ability, the researchers say.

in naming babies, parents unknowingly reference hurricanes

Baby names starting with *K*, such as Karl and Katie, became about **9% more popular** after Hurricane Katrina, evidence that parents' choices about what to call their children are influenced by the sound of names in the news, says a team led by Jonah Berger of The Wharton School. The more damaging, and thus the more prominent, a hurricane, the more popular are names containing sounds similar to the storm's designation. It's possible that commercial products also become more popular if their names sound like other things that have been prevalent recently, the researchers suggest.

toddlers cared for by grandma have lower scores

For every year that a young child spends being cared for by a grandmother or other relative while the mother works, his or her test scores at ages 3 to 6 **drop by 2.6%**, say Raquel Bernal of the Universidad de los Andes in Colombia and Michael P. Keane of the University of New South Wales. Formal, center-based child care has no such adverse effect on cognitive achievement, according to the study of more than 1,000 US single mothers and their children. Prior research suggests that grandparents are often stressed by child care and may not provide adequate educational activity.

a little music training in childhood goes a long way

Learning about rhythm, pitch, and melody for 20 days increased preschoolers' verbal-intelligence scores by an average of about **20%**, with more than **90%** of the children showing improvement, according to a study led by Sylvain Moreno of the Rotman Research Institute in Toronto. Music and language appear to be closely linked in the brain: the processing of music may overlap with mechanisms for handling other cognitive activities, the researchers say. A comparable training program in visual art yielded no improvement in verbal intelligence.

yes, college admissions officers do look at facebook

35% of US college admissions officers who went online to investigate candidates found evidence that hurt an applicant's chances of acceptance, according to a survey by Kaplan Test Prep. Offenses included plagiarism, illegal activities, and obscenities in blog posts. About **one-quarter** of admissions officers say they sometimes check Google or Facebook to find out more about applicants.

younger classmates perform better

Younger university students outperform their older classmates by **0.6%** to **3.3%** for each 11 months of age difference, according to Michele Pellizzari and Francesco Billari of Bocconi University in Italy. One reason may be that the youngest students in a given cohort tend to be smaller and thus less socially active, giving them more time to devote to studying, the researchers say.

fatalism makes people avoid preparing for retirement

Each **1-point** increase in workers' fatalism, the belief that they have little control over things, decreases their likelihood of making retirement calculations by **9%**, say Joel Shapiro of the University of Oxford and Stephen Wu of Hamilton College. Each **1-point increase** (along a 4-point scale) also decreases the probability of their reading about retirement by **6.7%**. To encourage retirement planning, policy makers should combat fatalism by persuading people that they really *do* have control over their future well-being, the researchers say. Some **11%** of the population is fatalistic, according to one study.

getting a bonus increases your chance of dying that week

You have a slightly higher chance of dying in the days after you get a paycheck or bonus, say William N. Evans of the University of Notre Dame and Timothy J. Moore of the University of Maryland. For example, during the week when the 2001 US tax rebate checks arrived, mortality among 25-to-64-year-olds increased by **2.5%**, and during the week when dividends are paid to Alaskans from the state's Permanent Fund, mortality increases by **13%**. Higher levels of activity such as driving and recreation after money rolls in are the likely causes of the effect, the authors say.

stats you can use

This wouldn't be a *Harvard Business Review* book if it didn't offer advice you could immediately apply to your own business problems. The findings in this chapter show how you can become more credible, what you need to do to get consumers to spend more, and where you should sit during lunch tomorrow. And where to put that spoon in your next ad.

consumers must have the same brand salsa for their chips

When simultaneously using multiple items, consumers prefer products of the same brand, a phenomenon that overwhelms their preexisting brand preferences. Research participants who were consuming a nonfavored brand (of chips, say) chose the same brand of a complementary product (salsa, for example) over a favored brand **more than 60%** of the time, on average, across 4 product categories, say doctoral student Ryan Rahinel and Joseph P. Redden of the University of Minnesota. People seem to believe that products under the same brand umbrella are somehow designed to go well together, the researchers say.

sometimes it's a bad idea to let customers complain

Giving customers a chance to complain about a product can be a bad idea if they believe its failure was their fault. Research subjects who thought a food processor was to blame for their failure to make a mango smoothie rated the machine higher (**4.02** versus **3** on a 9-point scale) after getting a chance to gripe to the company about it, but those who believed the failure was their fault rated the item lower (**3.29** versus **4.31**) after getting the same opportunity, say doctoral student Lea Dunn and Darren W. Dahl of the University of British Columbia. Because the effect was mitigated when participants were prompted to think about themselves positively, it might be beneficial for companies to frame requests for feedback in an affirmative manner, the researchers say.

when consumers feel special, they buy

In an experiment that provided participants with an opportunity to buy a discounted coffee mug, those who were told they had been randomly selected to get the discount were **3 times more** likely to want to buy than people who believed everyone got the discount. Researchers Jerry M. Burger and David F. Caldwell of Santa Clara University say such "special" opportunities may be appealing because people's self-esteem is tied to factors that distinguish them from the crowd.

be more credible by stating your promise in fine-grained numbers

Research participants predicted that a battery touted to last up to "2 hours" would function for just **89 minutes**, but they believed, on average, that a battery with life up to "120 minutes" would last **106 minutes**, say doctoral candidate Y. Charles Zhang and Norbert Schwarz of the University of Michigan. Consumers are more likely to believe that a company or product will deliver on its promise when the promise is conveyed in fine-grained rather than coarse units, the researchers say.

people will do more to help a group

Donations to save endangered butterflies were **69% higher** if the insects were shown flying in rows and beating their wings in unison rather than flying in a disorganized fashion, according to an experiment led by Robert W. Smith, a doctoral student at the University of Michigan. When victims are perceived to be a unit with a single identity, they evoke greater emotional concern from observers, the research suggests. Charities might be able to take advantage of this bias by presenting victims as coherent social groups and showing them behaving in a unified manner, the researchers say.

the product in the center of the shelf is the winner

In a study that involved fictitious brands of vitamins and energy drinks, a team led by A. Selin Atalay of HEC Paris found that a brand got longer looks and was more likely to be chosen when it was in the center of a horizontal product array (**44.4%**) than at the left (**23.8%**) or right (**31.7%**). Past research has shown that when exposed to a symmetric image, people have a propensity to look longer at the axis of symmetry.

when the rule is "pay what you want," almost everyone pays

Over the course of 2 years, only **0.5%** of patrons took advantage of the opportunity to eat for free at the pay-what-you-want Wiener Deewan self-service Pakistani restaurant in Vienna, Austria, say Gerhard Riener of the University of Jena and Christian Traxler of the University of Marburg, both in Germany. Over the course of 2 years, customer payments stabilized at an average of **€5**, well above the restaurant's costs, while the number of daily guests increased by more than **50%**, boosting revenue. The restaurant also benefited from fixed prices for drinks.

much-loved products often sell for less, not more

It's usually assumed that a person who is attached to a possession will demand a premium when it's sold, but the opposite often happens. The number of car owners who would consider selling their car at a 15% discount increased by **46%** if a prospective buyer professed an interest in restoring cars as opposed to stripping them, say Aaron R. Brough of Pepperdine University and Mathew S. Isaac of Seattle University. Greater attachment on the seller's part leads to greater sensitivity to the buyer's usage intentions.

if your ad shows a spoon, put it on the right side

When research subjects were shown a picture of a bowl of yogurt along with a spoon that was on the side matching their dominant hand (right side for righties), they reported being about **29% more** likely to buy the yogurt than when the spoon was on the other side, according to research by Ryan S. Elder of Brigham Young University and Aradhna Krishna of the University of Michigan. Seeing the spoon in a position where they could readily pick it up made it easier for participants to imagine using it, which heightened their purchase intentions. Because most people are right-handed, ads showing items that people can pick up should be oriented toward the right, the researchers say.

expensive things seem less valuable if they're bundled with cheap items

The fraction of people choosing a home gym over a 1-year gym membership dropped **31%** if the gym came bundled with a fitness DVD, a finding that pokes a hole in the notion that product value is always additive in the consumer's mind, according to an experiment by Aaron R. Brough of Pepperdine University and Alexander Chernev of Northwestern University. When trying to determine the value of a bundle of products with disparate prices, consumers tend to calculate a rough average rather than add the values of the items, the researchers suggest.

SCENARIO 1

49%
GYM
MEMBERSHIP

51%
HOME
GYM

SCENARIO 2

65%
GYM
MEMBERSHIP

35%
HOME GYM
+ DVD

When consumers were offered a choice between a gym membership and a home gym, slightly more than half preferred the home gym. But when a fitness DVD was included with the home gym, only about a third chose it.

workers consider training to be as valuable as a raise

Employer-provided training has the same effect on job satisfaction as a **17.7%** net wage increase, according to a study of nearly 5,000 workers in Spain by Santiago Budría of the University of Madeira. Other studies showing low productivity gains from training are overlooking the subjective benefits of on-the-job learning, Budría suggests.

fair treatment of retail workers leads to higher consumer spending

Even a small improvement in retail employees' sense that their company treats them fairly yields significant benefits: the employees perform better, and customers spend more money in stores. In a study of thousands of US employees and customers, a team of researchers led by James G. Maxham III of the University of Virginia found that a **1-point increase** on a 7-point scale of perceived organizational justice on employees' part led to customers' spending **$1.43 more** per person per visit.

smaller teams are quicker

Two-person teams took an average of just **36 minutes** to assemble 50 Lego pieces into a human figure, a task that required **52 minutes** for four-person teams, according to an experiment by Bradley R. Staats of the University of North Carolina, Katherine L. Milkman of Wharton, and Craig R. Fox of UCLA. Moreover, people consistently underestimate the additional time needed by larger teams, with the forecasting errors growing larger as teams get bigger. Increasing a team's size can hamper coordination, diminish members' motivation, and increase conflict, the researchers say.

to boost workers' productivity, tell them how they rank . . .

After a German wholesaler began privately informing its warehouse workers how they ranked among other employees on pay and performance, their average productivity **jumped 6.8%**, an effect that showed no signs of abating over the long term, say Jordi Blanes i Vidal and Mareike Nossol of the London School of Economics. The initiative, which didn't cost the company anything, suggests that providing information about employees' relative performance is unambiguously beneficial to a firm's profitability, the researchers say.

. . . yet for some, merely being ranked diminishes IQ

A group of participants suffered an average IQ drop of **17.4 points** during an experiment in which they were ranked by their intelligence scores, suggesting that simply being ranked can profoundly diminish some people's ability to express their cognitive ability, says a team led by Read Montague of Virginia Tech and University College London. Not everyone in the experiment responded this way; some participants' scores even improved. Individual differences in social sensitivity may play an important role in shaping intelligence, the researchers say.

you should sit with more people in the lunchroom

Workers who regularly sit with large groups of colleagues at tables for **10 or 12** in their lunchrooms have substantially **higher** performance than those who sit at tables for **4**, according to a CNN report on findings by researcher Ben Waber. Workers who sit with larger groups at lunch tend to be clued in to the work of greater numbers of colleagues and can tap more people for advice, Waber says.

154

moderate background noise can make you more creative . . .

Research participants were more creative when they were exposed to background noise of **70 decibels**, comparable to the sound of a moving car 10 meters away, than when they were in a low-noise environment, say Ravi Mehta of the University of Illinois, Rui (Juliet) Zhu of the University of British Columbia, and Amar Cheema of the University of Virginia. The noise makes mental processing more difficult, which activates abstract cognition and thus enhances creative performance, the researchers say.

. . . but coworkers' conversations can impair your performance

Overhearing your office mates' conversations can cause a decline of **5%** to **10%** in your ability to read, write, and carry out other tasks requiring efficient use of short-term memory, according to a *New York Times* report of a study by Finland's Institute of Occupational Health. The researchers found that in an office environment, speech is the most disturbing type of sound because it is processed by working memory. Employees perform better when speech is masked by the sound of a babbling brook.

to make a task seem easier, lean back a little

People who leaned back so that their eyes were an average of **38.8 inches** from a computer screen found the task of pronouncing meaningless strings of letters easier than people who leaned forward to **12.5 inches**, say Manoj Thomas of Cornell University and Claire I. Tsai of the University of Toronto. Increasing the physical distance from a complex task also increases the psychological distance, which mitigates the sense of the task's difficulty. The mind infers that a task seen from a greater distance is easier.

contradiction alert: extra thinking time leads to ethical decisions . . .

87% of research subjects opted not to lie for self-gain if they were given 3 minutes to contemplate their choice, compared with just **56%** of participants who were told to make an immediate decision, says a team led by J. Keith Murnighan of Northwestern University's Kellogg School. The researchers suggest that in companies with a "fast pulse" and a tendency to reward quick decision making, employees may make ethical missteps because they lack adequate time for contemplation.

158

... yet deliberation makes you more likely to cheat

According to a series of psychological experiments by Chen-Bo Zhong of the University of Toronto, **68.2%** of people who were in a deliberative mind-set were willing to lie for their own gain, compared with just **36.4%** of people who were thinking intuitively, suggesting that thoughtful deliberation poses a danger to moral judgment. Zhong questions whether traditional business education focuses too intently on cultivating a deliberative approach to decisions in managers.

the predictive power of the gut

Research participants who strongly trusted their feelings were able to predict future levels of the Dow Jones average with **25% greater** accuracy than people who didn't, says a team led by Michel Tuan Pham of Columbia Business School. In another experiment, **41%** of people who trusted their feelings were able to correctly pick an *American Idol* winner, compared with just **24%** of people with little trust in their feelings. Relying on a gut sense allows people to tap into the brain's unconscious syntheses of knowledge from many sources, the researchers say.

if you're a boss but have low status, give orders

Incoming leaders with low status are most effective when they "take charge"—a tactic that backfires for high-status incoming leaders. In the case of a new leader who was inexperienced and went to a second-tier business school, team members in an experiment by Stephen J. Sauer of Clarkson University gave an average effectiveness rating of **4.25** (on a 1-to-7 scale) if the leader told people what to do, but a rating of just **3.55** if the leader asked members their opinions. If the leader was more experienced and a graduate of a top-tier school, members gave the individual a **3.66** rating for telling people what to do and a **4.35** for soliciting opinions. People with high status are better off relying solely on their personal power to influence others, Sauer says.

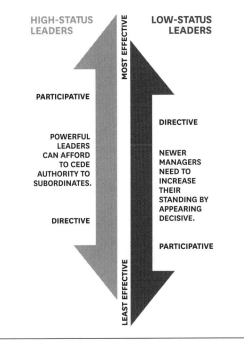

HIGH-STATUS
LEADERS

LOW-STATUS
LEADERS

MOST EFFECTIVE

LEAST EFFECTIVE

PARTICIPATIVE

POWERFUL
LEADERS
CAN AFFORD
TO CEDE
AUTHORITY TO
SUBORDINATES.

DIRECTIVE

DIRECTIVE

NEWER
MANAGERS
NEED TO
INCREASE
THEIR
STANDING BY
APPEARING
DECISIVE.

PARTICIPATIVE

Which leadership style is best? It depends on your status.

to be quicker and sharper, sniff peppermint

Students who were exposed to the scent of peppermint completed **4% more** levels in the Nintendo Wii Fit Plus Perfect 10 video game and scored **26% more** hits during the Snowball Fight game, according to a team led by Kristin McCombs of Wheeling Jesuit University. Peppermint also increased participants' physiological arousal and kept them more engaged in the game. Past research has shown that peppermint enhances attention, memory, alertness, and mood.

improve your golf game by thinking powerful thoughts

People who were primed to think of themselves as powerful sank **44% more** golf putts at 150 centimeters than their peers, according to Pascal Burgmer and Birte Englich of the University of Cologne in Germany. Moreover, people who saw high-power-related words such as "influence" embedded in a puzzle scored **29% higher** on a game of darts than people who saw low-power-related words such as "serve." Thoughts of possessing power appear to induce better perception of information that's relevant to goals, leading to improved motor performance in pursuit of those goals, the researchers suggest.

163

mimicking customers helps salespeople succeed

Retail salespeople who subtly mimic customers' speech and behavior are more successful at selling, according to an experiment led by Céline Jacob of the Université de Bretagne-Sud in France. Among customers who solicited salespeople for information about an MP3 player, **78.8%** bought such a product from mimickers, compared with **61.8%** from nonmimickers. Afterward, customers who had been mimicked were more positive about the salespeople and the store.

will karma help you get a job?

Job-fair attendees who were prompted to think about their lack of control over their employment prospects offered to donate **67% more** money to a charity than other attendees, an indication that people are inclined to do good deeds to try to improve their fortunes, according to a study by Benjamin A. Converse of the University of Virginia and Jane L. Risen and Travis J. Carter of the University of Chicago. People who made these kinds of investments in "karma" were more optimistic about getting what they wanted, the researchers say.

165

to be truly happy, be a boss in a small company

People who work for small organizations are about **25% more** likely to be happy than those toiling in large organizations of 1,000 employees or more, according to early results of a survey of visitors to Delivering Happiness at Work, cofounded by Zappos CEO Tony Hsieh. Among the other findings: supervising others (as opposed to being supervised) is associated with more happiness.

sources

1. Pettit, Nathan C., and Niro Sivanathan. "The Eyes and Ears of Status: How Status Colors Perceptual Judgment." *Personality and Social Psychology Bulletin* 38, no. 5 (May 2012): 570–582.

2. Duguid, Michelle M., and Jack A. Goncalo. "Living Large: The Powerful Overestimate Their Own Height." *Psychological Science* 23, no. 1 (January 2012): 36–40.

3. "Tough or Handsome? The Difference Can Turn on a (Close) Haircut." *Wall Street Journal*, July 23, 2012.

4. Di Muro, Fabrizio, and Theodore J. Noseworthy. "Money Isn't Everything, but It Helps If It Doesn't Look Used: How the Physical Appearance of Money Influences Spending." *Journal of Consumer Research* 39, no. 6 (2013): 1330–1342.

5. Bastian, Brock, Jolanda Jetten, and Elizabeth Stewart. "Physical Pain and Guilty Pleasures." *Social Psychological and Personality Science* 4, no. 2 (March 2013): 215–219.

6. Doerrfeld, Adam, Natalie Sebanz, and Maggie Shiffrar. "Expecting to lift a box together makes the load look lighter." *Psychological Research* 76, no. 4 (July 2012): 467–475.

7. Lichtenfeld, Stephanie, Andrew J Elliot, Markus A Maier, and Reinhard Pekrun, "Fertile Green: Green Facilitates Creative Performance." *Personality and Social Psychology Bulletin* 38, no. 6 (June 2012): 784–797.

8. Bagchi, Rajesh, and Amar Cheema. "The Effect of Red Background Color on Willingness-to-Pay: The Moderating

Role of Selling Mechanism." *Journal of Consumer Research* 39, no. 5 (February 2013): 947–960.

9. Guéguen, Nicolas, and Céline Jacob. "Clothing Color and Tipping: Gentlemen Patrons Give More Tips to Waitresses with Red Clothes." *Journal of Hospitality & Tourism Research*, April 18, 2012.

10. Roussanov, Nikolai L., and Pavel G. Savor. "Status, Marriage, and Managers' Attitudes to Risk." Paper presented at AFA 2013 San Diego Meetings, December 14, 2012. http://ssrn.com/abstract=1787381 or http://dx.doi.org/10.2139/ssrn.1787381.

11. Chae, Boyoun (Grace), and JoAndrea Hoegg. "The Future Looks 'Right': Effects of the Horizontal Location of Advertising Images on Product Attitude." *Journal of Consumer Research*.

12. Gervais, Will M., Azim F. Shariff, and Ara Norenzayan. "Do you believe in atheists? Distrust is central to anti-atheist prejudice." *Journal of Personality and Social Psychology* 101, no 6 (December 2011): 1189–1206.

13. Simonsohn, Uri. "Weather to Go to College." *Economic Journal* 120, no. 543 (March 2010): 270–280.

14. Hong, Jiewen, and Yacheng Sun. "Warm It Up with Love: The Effect of Physical Coldness on Liking of Romance Movies." *Journal of Consumer Research* 39, no. 2 (August 2012): 293–306.

15. Wiltermuth, Scott S., and Margaret A. Neale. "Too Much Information: The Perils of Nondiagnostic Information in Negotiations." *Journal of Applied Psychology* 96, no. 1 (January 2011): 192–201.

16. DeVoe, Sanford E., and Julian House. "Time, money, and happiness: How does putting a price on time affect our ability to smell the roses?" *Journal of Experimental Social Psychology* 48, no. 2 (March 2012): 466–474.

17. Sanders, Matthew A., Steve D. Shirk, Chris J. Burgin, and Leonard L. Martin. "The Gargle Effect: Rinsing the Mouth with Glucose Enhances Self-Control." *Psychological Science* 23, no. 12 (December 2012): 1470–1472.

18. Sulloway, Frank J., and Richard L. Zweigenhaft. "Birth Order and Risk Taking in Athletics: A Meta-Analysis and Study of Major League Baseball." *Personality & Social Psychology Review* 14, no. 4 (November 2010): 402–416.

19. Han, Seunghee, Jennifer Lerner, and Richard Zeckhauser. "The disgust-promotes-disposal effect." *Journal of Risk & Uncertainty* 44, no. 2 (April 2012): 101–113.

20. Lee, Spike W. S., and Norbert Schwarz. "Bidirectionality, Mediation, and Moderation of Metaphorical Effects: The Embodiment of Social Suspicion and Fishy Smells." *Journal of Personality & Social Psychology* 103, no. 5 (November 2012): 737–749.

21. Burns, Ronald, Patrick Kinkade, and Michael Bachmann. "Getting hosed: Petty theft in the car wash industry and the fifth suitability criterion in routine activities theory." *Social Science Journal* 49, no. 3 (September 2012): 263–269.

22. Ruderman, Wendy. "414 Homicides in '12 Is a Record Low for New York City." *New York Times*. http://www.nytimes.com/2012/12/29/nyregion/414-homicides-is-a-record-low-for-new-york.html.

23. Song, Xuguang, and Wenhao Cheng. "Perception of Corruption in 36 Major Chinese Cities: Based on Survey of 1,642 Experts." *Social Indicators Research* 109, no. 2 (November 2012): 211–221.

24. Gino, Francesca, and Adam D. Galinsky. "Vicarious dishonesty: When psychological closeness creates distance from one's moral compass." *Organizational Behavior & Human Decision Processes* 119, no. 1 (September 2012): 15–26.

25. Epting, L. Kimberly, Kristen N. Riggs, Joseph D. Knowles, and John J. Hanky. "Cheers vs. Jeers: Effects of

Audience Feedback on Individual Athletic Performance." *North American Journal of Psychology* 13, no. 2 (2011): 299–312.

26. Baumann, Robert, and Bryan Engelhardt. "Crime and the Decline of Unions." *LABOUR: Review of Labour Economics & Industrial Relations* 26, no. 2 (June 2012): 225–234.

27. "Financial Services Professionals Feel Unethical Behavior May Be a Necessary Evil and Have Knowledge of Workplace Misconduct." Labaton Sucharow Survey, July 10, 2012. http://www.labaton.com/en/about/press/Labaton-Sucharow-announces-results-of-financial-services-professional-survey.cfm.

28. Hussey, Andrew. "The effect of ethics on labor market success: Evidence from MBAs." *Journal of Economic Behavior & Organization* 80, no. 1 (September 2011): 168–180.

29. Bhattacharya, Utpal, and Cassandra D. Marshall. "Do They Do It for the Money?" *CFA Digest* 42, no. 2 (May 2012): 121–123.

30. Townsend, Claudia, and Wendy Liu. "Is Planning Good for You? The Differential Impact of Planning on Self-Regulation." *Journal of Consumer Research* 39, no. 4 (December 2012): 688–703.

31. Maag, Christopher, "The Scary Consequences of a Lost Smartphone." March 3, 2012. http://www.credit.com/blog/2012/03/the-scary-consequences-of-a-lost-smartphone/.

32. Norton, Elizabeth. "Shame on the Rich." February 27, 2012. http://news.sciencemag.org/sciencenow/2012/02/shame-on-the-rich.html.

33. Zimbler, Mattitiyahu, and Robert S. Feldman. "Liar, Liar, Hard Drive on Fire: How Media Context Affects Lying Behavior." *Journal of Applied Social Psychology* 41, no. 10 (October 2011): 2492–2507.

34. Hackl, Franz, Martin Halla, and Gerald J. Pruckner. "Volunteering and the state." *Public Choice* 151, no. 3/4 (June 2012): 465–495.

35. Habyarimana, James, and William Jack. "Heckle and Chide: Results of a randomized road safety intervention in

Kenya." *Journal of Public Economics* 95, no. 11/12 (December 2011): 1438–1446.

36. Zak, Paul J. "The physiology of moral sentiments." *Journal of Economic Behavior & Organization* 77, no. 1 (January 2011): 53–65.

37. Carrell, Scott E., Mark Hoekstra, and James E. West. "Does drinking impair college performance? Evidence from a regression discontinuity approach." *Journal of Public Economics* 95, no. 1/2 (February 2011): 54–62.

38. Eskine, Kendall J. "Wholesome Foods and Wholesome Morals? Organic Foods Reduce Prosocial Behavior and Harshen Moral Judgments." *Social Psychological and Personality Science* 4 no. 2 (March 2013): 251–254.

39. DeWall, Nathan C. "Hurt Feelings? You Could Take a Pain Reliever …" *Harvard Business Review* 89, no. 4 (April 2011): 28–29.

40. Kwon, Youngsun, Seung Hun Han, and Changi Nam. "Estimating the costs of political populism: Traffic violation pardons in Korea." *Transportation Research Part A: Policy & Practice* 46, no. 9 (November 2012): 1449–1457.

41. Lindo, Jason M. "Parental job loss and infant health." *Journal of Health Economics* 30, no. 5 (September 2011): 869–879.

42. Herbst, Chris M. "'Paradoxical' decline? Another look at the relative reduction in female happiness." *Journal of Economic Psychology* 32, no. 5 (October 2011): 773–788.

43. Kraft, Tara L., and Sarah D. Pressman. "Grin and Bear It: The Influence of Manipulated Facial Expression on the Stress Response." *Psychological Science* 23, no. 11 (November 2012): 1372–1378.

44. Daly, Mary C., Andrew J. Oswald, Daniel Wilson, and Stephen Wu. "Dark contrasts: The paradox of high rates of suicide in happy places." *Journal of Economic Behavior & Organization* 80, no. 3 (December 2011): 435–442.

45. Colman, Gregory J., and Dhaval M. Dave. "Exercise, Physical Activity, and Exertion over the Business Cycle." NBER

Working Paper No. 17406, September 2011. http://www.nber
.org/papers/w17406.

46. Schwartz, Janet, Jason Riis, Brian Elbel, and Dan
Ariely. "Inviting Consumers to Downsize Fast-Food Portions
Significantly Reduces Calorie Consumption." *Health Affairs* 31,
no. 2 (February 2012): 399–407.

47. Dubois, David, Derek D. Rucker, and Adam D.
Galinsky. "Super Size Me: Product Size as a Signal of Status."
Journal of Consumer Research 38, no. 6 (April 2012): 1047–1062.

48. Jacobson, Sheldon H., Douglas M. King, and Rong
Yuan. "A note on the relationship between obesity and driving."
Transport Policy 18, no. 5 (September 2011): 772–776.

49. Crozier, Thomas W. M., Angelique Stalmach, Michael
E. J. Lean, and Alan Crozier. "Espresso coffees, caffeine and
chlorogenic acid intake: potential health implications." *Food &
Function* 3, no. 30: (2012).

50. Wagner, David T., Christopher M. Barnes, Vivien
K. G. Lim, and D. Lance Ferri. "Lost Sleep and Cyberloafing:
Evidence from the Laboratory and a Daylight Saving Time
Quasi-Experiment." *Journal of Applied Psychology* 97, no. 5
(September 2012): 1068–1076.

51. Souitaris, Vangelis, and B. M. Marcello Maestro. "The
Case for Multitasking." *Harvard Business Review* 89, no. 10
(October 2011): 32–32.

52. Raghubir, Priya, Vicki G. Morwitz, and Amitav
Chakravarti. "Spatial categorization and time perception:
Why does it take less time to get home?" *Journal of Consumer
Psychology* 21, no. 2 (April 2011): 192–198.

53. van Ommeren, Jos N., and Eva Gutiérrez-i-Puigarnau.
"Are workers with a long commute less productive? An
empirical analysis of absenteeism." *Regional Science & Urban
Economics* 41, no. 1 (January 2011): 1–8.

54. Dutcher, E. Glenn. "The effects of telecommut-
ing on productivity: An experimental examination. The role

of dull and creative tasks." *Journal of Economic Behavior & Organization* 84, no. 1 (2012): 355–363.

55. Hussey, Andrew. "Human Capital Augmentation Versus the Signaling Value of MBA Education." *Economics of Education Review* 31, no. 4 (August 2012): 442–451.

56. Bonezzi, Andrea, C. Miguel Brendl, and Matteo de Angelis. "Stuck in the Middle: The Psychophysics of Goal Pursuit." *Psychological Science* 22, no. 5 (May 2011): 607–612.

57. Robinson, John P., Steven Martin, Ignace Glorieux, and Joeri Minnen. "The overestimated workweek revisited." *Monthly Labor Review* 134, no. 6 (June 2011): 43–53.

58. Manjoo, Farhad. "The Happiness Machine: How Google Became Such a Great Place to Work." *Slate*, January 21, 2013. http://www.slate.com/articles/technology/technology/2013/01/google_people_operations_the_secrets_of_the_world_s_most_scientific_human.html.

59. Silverman, Rachel Emma. "Where's the Boss? Trapped in a Meeting." *Wall Street Journal*, February 13, 2012. http://finance.yahoo.com/news/where-s-the-boss--trapped-in-a-meeting.html.

60. Park, Sun Hyun, James D. Westphal, and Ithai Stern. "Set up for a Fall: The Insidious Effects of Flattery and Opinion Conformity toward Corporate Leaders." *Administrative Science Quarterly* 56, no. 2 (June 2011): 257–302.

61. Saffer, Henry, and Karine Lamiraud. "The effect of hours of work on social interaction." *Review of Economics of the Household* 10, no. 2 (June 2012): 237–258.

62. Gouveia, Aaron. "Do Americans Still Value Hard Work?" Salary.com. http://www.salary.com/does-america-still-value-work/.

63. Silverman, Rachel Emma, and Robin Sidel. "Warming Up to the Officeless Office." *Wall Street Journal*, April 17, 2012. http://online.wsj.com/article/SB10001424052702304818404577349783161465976.html.

64. Clifton, Jim. "What Makes Workplaces Miserable." Gallup.com, March 28, 2012. http://thechairmansblog.gallup.com/2012/03/what-makes-workplaces-miserable.html.

65. Mulvey, Jeanette. "What Workers Really Do on 'Sick Days.'" *BusinessNewsDaily*, March 27, 2012. http://www.businessnewsdaily.com/2260-workers-sick-days.html.

66. Griskevicius, Vladas, Joshua M. Ackerman, Joshua M. Tybur, Andrew W. Delton, Theresa E. Robertson, and Andrew E. White. "The Financial Consequences of Too Many Men: Sex Ratio Effects on Saving, Borrowing, and Spending." *Journal of Personality & Social Psychology* 102, no. 1 (January 2012): 69–80.

67. Judge, Timothy A., Beth A. Livingston, and Charlice Hurst. "Do Nice Guys—and Gals—Really Finish Last? The Joint Effects of Sex and Agreeableness on Income." *Journal of Personality & Social Psychology* 102, no. 2 (February 2012): 390–407.

68. Chang, Alicia, Catherine M. Sandhofer, and Christia S. Brown. "Gender Biases in Early Number Exposure to Preschool-Aged Children." *Journal of Language & Social Psychology* 30, no. 4 (December 2011): 440–450.

69. Bauernschuster, Stefan, and Helmut Rainer. "Political regimes and the family: how sex-role attitudes continue to differ in reunified Germany." *Journal of Population Economics* 25, no. 1 (December 2011): 5–27.

70. Peterson, Kristina. "How a Male CEO's Kids Affect His Workers' Pay." *Wall Street Journal*, January 6, 2013, http://online.wsj.com/article/SB10001424127887324391104578225710891707312.html.

71. Buser, Thomas. "The impact of the menstrual cycle and hormonal contraceptives on competitiveness." *Journal of Economic Behavior & Organization* 83, no. 1 (June 2012): 1–10.

72. Betz, Diana E., and Denise Sekaquaptewa. "My Fair Physicist? Feminine Math and Science Role Models Demotivate Young Girls." *Social Psychological and Personality Science* 3, no. 6 (November 2012): 738–746.

73. "Behind the Boss: A Peek at Company Leaders' Personal Style." CareerBuilder. http://www.careerbuilder.com/JobPoster/Resources/page.aspx?pagever=2011SeniorLevelHabits&template=none&sc_cmp2=JP_Infographic_2011SeniorLevelHabits.

74. Coles, Melvyn G., and Marco Francesconi. "On the Emergence of Toyboys: The Timing of Marriage with Aging and Uncertain Careers." *International Economic Review* 52, no. 3 (August 2011): 825–853.

75. Martin, Brett A. S. "A Stranger's Touch: Effects of Accidental Interpersonal Touch on Consumer Evaluations and Shopping Time." *Journal of Consumer Research* 39, no. 1 (June 2012): 174–184.

76. Kalil, Ariel, Magne Mogstad, Mari Rege, and Mark Votruba. "Divorced Fathers' Proximity and Children's Long-Run Outcomes: Evidence from Norwegian Registry Data." *Demography* 48, no. 3 (August 2011): 1005–1027.

77. Krogstrup, Signe, and Sébastien Wälti. "Women and Budget Deficits." *Scandinavian Journal of Economics* 113, no. 3 (2011): 712–728.

78. Gaskell, Adi. "Commuting Stresses More Women Than Men." *Technorati*, August 23, 2011. http://technorati.com/women/article/commuting-stresses-more-women-than-men1/.

79. Benard, Stephen. "Why His Merit Raise Is Bigger Than Hers." *Harvard Business Review* 90, no. 4 (April 2012): 26–26.

80. Kosteas, Vasilios. "The Effect of Exercise on Earnings: Evidence from the NLSY." *Journal of Labor Research* 33, no. 2 (June 2012): 225–250.

81. Cheng, Ping, Zhenguo Lin, and Yingchun Liu. "Do Women Pay More for Mortgages?" *Journal of Real Estate Finance & Economics* 43, no. 4 (November 2011): 423–444.

82. "Conservative management trumps political ideology, as companies headed by Republicans pay more tax than those led by Democrats." American Accounting Association. http://aaahq.org/newsroom/ConservativeMgmtTrumps_07_06_12.htm.

83. "New Business Startups Declined in 2011, Annual Study Shows." Ewing Marion Kauffman Foundation, March 19, 2012. http://www.kauffman.org/newsroom/annual-new-business-startups-study.aspx.

84. Kalil, Ariel, and Patrick Wightman. "Parental Job Loss and Children's Educational Attainment in Black and White Middle-Class Families." *Social Science Quarterly* 92, no. 1 (March 2011): 57–78.

85. Heywood, John S., and Daniel Parent. "Performance Pay and the White-Black Wage Gap." *Journal of Labor Economics* 30, no. 2 (April 2012): 249–290.

86. "GE Feels Its Own Cuts." *Wall Street Journal*, September 17, 2012. http://online.wsj.com/article/SB10000872 3963904437202045780022702224345846.html.

87. Williams, Alex. "Just Wait Until Your Mother Gets Home." *New York Times*, August 10, 2012, http://www.nytimes.com/2012/08/12/fashion/dads-are-taking-over-as-full-time-parents.html.

88. Christafore, David, and Susane Leguizamon. "The influence of gay and lesbian coupled households on house prices in conservative and liberal neighborhoods." *Journal of Urban Economics* 71, no. 2 (March 2012): 258–267.

89. Cummings, Rocky B., and Joseph Carr. "Holiday Gift Card Season Is Upon Us—Has Your State Been Naughty or Nice?" *Journal of State Taxation* 31, no. 1 (November–December 2012): 7–45.

90. Pfau, Wade D. "Will 2000-Era Retirees Experience the Worst Retirement Outcomes in U.S. History? A Progress Report after 10 Years." *Journal of Investing* 20, no. 4 (Winter 2011): 117–131.

91. Herbst, Chris M. "'Paradoxical' decline? Another look at the relative reduction in female happiness." *Journal of Economic Psychology* 32, no. 5 (October 2011): 773–788.

92. Conyon, Martin J., and Lerong He. "Executive compensation and corporate governance in China." *Journal of Corporate Finance* 17, no. 4 (September 2011): 1158–1175.

93. Chozick, Amy. "As Young Lose Interest in Cars, G.M. Turns to MTV for Help." *New York Times*, March 22, 2012. http://www.nytimes.com/2012/03/23/business/media/to-draw-reluctant-young-buyers-gm-turns-to-mtv.html.

94. Censky, Annalyn. "Why the Jobs Recovery Favors Single Workers." *CNNMoney*, August 16, 2012. http://money.cnn.com/2012/08/15/news/economy/jobs-single-workers/index.html.

95. Kumar, Alok, Jeremy K. Page, and Oliver G. Spalt. "Religious beliefs, gambling attitudes, and financial market outcomes." *Journal of Financial Economics* 102, no. 3 (December 2011): 671–708.

96. Do, Chau, and Irina Paley. "Altruism from the house: the impact of home equity on charitable giving." *Review of Economics of the Household* 10, no. 3 (September 2012): 375–393.

97. Kamakura, Wagner A., and Rex Yuxing Du. "How Economic Contractions and Expansions Affect Expenditure Patterns." *Journal of Consumer Research* 39, no. 2 (August 2012): 229–247.

98. Matsa, David A. "Competition and Product Quality in the Supermarket Industry." *Quarterly Journal of Economics* 126, no. 3 (August 2011): 1539–1591.

99. Levitt, Steven D., and Thomas J. Miles. "The Role of Skill Versus Luck in Poker: Evidence from the World Series of Poker." *Journal of Sports Economics*, June 22, 2012.

100. Feldmann, Horst. "The Unemployment Puzzle of Corporate Taxation." *Public Finance Review* 39, no. 6 (November 2011): 743–769.

101. Li, Norman P., Lily Patel, Daniel Balliet, William Tov, and Christie Scollon. "The Incompatibility of Materialism and the Desire for Children: Psychological Insights into the Fertility Discrepancy Among Modern Countries." *Social Indicators Research* 101, no. 3 (May 2011): 391–404.

102. Bruns, Christian, and Oliver Himmler. "Newspaper Circulation and Local Government Efficiency." *Scandinavian Journal of Economics* 113, no. 2 (2011): 470–492.

103. Feldman, Todd. "The Most Destructive Behavioral Bias." *Journal of Investing* 21, no. 2 (Summer 2012): 49–56.

104. McCartney, Scott. "How Airlines Spend Your Airfare." *Wall Street Journal*, June 6, 2012. http://online.wsj.com/article/SB10001424052702303296604577450581396602106.html?KEYWORDS=how+airlines+spend+your+airfare.

105. Berger, Jonah, and Devin Pope. "Can Losing Lead to Winning?" *Management Science* 57, no. 5 (May 2011): 817–827.

106. Gaissmaier, Wolfgang, and Gerd Gigerenzer. "9/11, Act II: A Fine-Grained Analysis of Regional Variations in Traffic Fatalities in the Aftermath of the Terrorist Attacks." *Psychological Science* 23, no. 12 (December 2012): 1449–1454.

107. Lin, Chen, Micah S. Officer, and Hong Zou. "Directors' and officers' liability insurance and acquisition outcomes." *Journal of Financial Economics* 102, no. 3 (December 2011): 507–525.

108. Kavetsos, Georgios, and Pantelis Koutroumpis. "Technological affluence and subjective well-being." *Journal of Economic Psychology* 32, no. 5 (October 2011): 742–753.

109. Cronqvist, Henrik, Anil K. Makhija, and Scott E. Yonker. "Behavioral consistency in corporate finance: CEO personal and corporate leverage." *Journal of Financial Economics* 103, no. 1 (January 2012): 20–40.

110. Budría, Santiago. "The shadow value of employer-provided training." *Journal of Economic Psychology* 33, no. 3 (June 2012): 494–514.

111. Lubian, Diego, and Luca Zarri. "Happiness and tax morale: An empirical analysis." *Journal of Economic Behavior & Organization* 80, no. 1 (September 2011): 223–243.

112. Sussman, Abigail, and Christopher Y. Olivola. "Axe the Tax: Taxes Are Disliked More than Equivalent Costs." *Journal of Marketing Research* 48 (October 2011): S91–S101.

113. Dey, Aiyesha, Ellen Engel, and Xiaohui Liu. "CEO and board chair roles: To split or not to split?" *Journal of Corporate Finance* 17, no. 5 (December 2011): 1595–1618.

114. Gao, Huasheng, Jarrad Harford, and Kai Li. "CEO Pay Cuts and Forced Turnover: Their Causes and Consequences." *CFA Digest* 42, no. 3 (August 2012): 32–34.

115. Simmons, Joseph P., Leif D. Nelson, and Uri Simonsohn. "False-Positive Psychology: Undisclosed Flexibility in Data Collection and Analysis Allows Presenting Anything as Significant." *Psychological Science* 22, no. 11 (November 2011): 1359–1366.

116. Glisson, William, Tim Storer, Gavin Mayall, Iain Moug, and George Grispos. "Electronic retention: What does your mobile phone reveal about you?" *International Journal of Information Security* 10, no. 6 (November 2011): 337–349.

117. Kortt, Michael A., and Brian Dollery. "Religion and the rate of return to human capital: Evidence from Australia." *Applied Economics Letters* 19, no. 10 (July 2012): 943–946.

118. Christensen, Finn. "The pill and partnerships: The impact of the birth control pill on cohabitation." *Journal of Population Economics* 25, no. 1 (December 2011): 29–52.

119. Vespa, Jonathan, and Matthew Painter. "Cohabitation History, Marriage, and Wealth Accumulation." *Demography* 48, no. 3 (August 2011): 983–1004.

120. Miron-Spektor, Ella, Miriam Erez, and Eitan Naveh. "To Drive Creativity, Add Some Conformity." *Harvard Business Review* 90, no. 3 (March 2012): 30.

121. Bauman, Yoram, and Elaina Rose. "Selection or indoctrination: Why do economics students donate less than the rest?" *Journal of Economic Behavior & Organization* 79, no. 3 (August 2011): 318–327.

122. Zaigraev, Grigorii G. "Alcoholism and Drunkenness in Russia." *Sociological Research* 49, no. 6 (November–December 2010): 3–18.

123. "AICPA Survey: Finances Causing Rifts for American Couples." AICPA, May 4, 2012. http://www.aicpa.org/press/pressreleases/2012/pages/finances-causing-rifts-for-american-couples.aspx.

124. Macunovich, Diane. "The role of demographics in precipitating economic downturns." *Journal of Population Economics* 25, no. 3 (July 2012): 783–807.

125. Tirunillai, Seshadri, and Gerard J. Tellis. "Does Chatter Really Matter? Dynamics of User-Generated Content and Stock Performance." *Marketing Science* 31, no. 2 (March–April 2012): 198–215.

126. Wong, Elaine M., Margaret E. Ormiston, and Michael P. Haselhuhn. "A Face Only an Investor Could Love: CEOs' Facial Structure Predicts Their Firms' Financial Performance." *Psychological Science* 22, no. 12 (December 2011): 1478–1483.

127. Taha, Nadia. "The Cost, in Dollars, of Raising a Child." *New York Times*, November 13, 2012. http://bucks.blogs.nytimes.com/2012/11/13/the-cost-in-dollars-of-raising-a-child/.

128. Frenette, Marc. "Why do larger families reduce parental investments in child quality, but not child quality per se?" *Review of Economics of the Household* 9, no. 4 (December 2011): 523–537.

129. Mungai, Edward, and S. Ramakrishna Velamuri. "Parental Entrepreneurial Role Model Influence on Male Offspring: Is It Always Positive and When Does It Occur?" *Entrepreneurship: Theory & Practice* 35, no. 2 (March 2011): 337–357.

130. Brown, Sarah, Aurora Ortiz-Nunez, and Karl Taylor. "Parental Risk Attitudes and Children's Academic Test Scores: Evidence from the US Panel Study of Income Dynamics." *Scottish Journal of Political Economy* 59, no. 1 (February 2012): 47–70.

131. Berger, Jonah, Eric T. Bradlow, Alex Braunstein, and Yao Zhang. "From Karen to Katie: Using Baby Names to Understand Cultural Evolution." *Psychological Science* 23, no. 10 (October 2012): 1067–1073.

132. Bernal, Raquel, and Michael P. Keane. "Child Care Choices and Children's Cognitive Achievement: The Case of

Single Mothers." *Journal of Labor Economics* 29, no. 3 (July 2011): 459–512.

133. Moreno, Sylvain, Ellen Bialystok, Raluca Barac, E. Glenn Schellenberg, Nicholas J. Cepeda, and Tom Chau. "Short-Term Music Training Enhances Verbal Intelligence and Executive Function." *Psychological Science* 22, no. 11 (November 2011): 1425–1433.

134. "Kaplan Test Prep Survey Finds That College Admissions Officers' Discovery of Online Material Damaging to Applicants Nearly Triples in a Year." Kaplan Test Prep Online, October 4, 2012. http://press.kaptest.com/press-releases/kaplan-test-prep-survey-finds-that-college-admissions-officers-discovery-of-on-line-material-damaging-to-applicants-nearly-triples-in-a-year.

135. Pellizzari, Michele, and Francesco Billari. "The younger, the better? Age-related differences in academic performance at university." *Journal of Population Economics* 25, no. 2 (January 2012): 697–739.

136. Shapiro, Joel, and Stephen Wu. "Fatalism and Savings." *Journal of Socio-Economics* 40, no. 5 (October 2011): 645–651.

137. Evans, William N., and Timothy J. Moore. "The short-term mortality consequences of income receipt." *Journal of Public Economics* 95, no. 11/12 (December 2011): 1410–1424.

138. Rahinel, Ryan, and Joseph P. Redden. "Brands as Product Coordinators: Matching Brands Make Joint Consumption Experiences More Enjoyable." *Journal of Consumer Research* 39, no. 6 (April 2013): 1290–1299.

139. Dunn, Lea, and Darren W. Dahl. "Self-Threat and Product Failure: How Internal Attributions of Blame Affect Consumer Complaining Behavior." *Journal of Marketing Research* 49, no. 5 (October 2012): 670–681.

140. Burger, Jerry M., and David F. Caldwell. "When opportunity knocks: The effect of a perceived unique opportunity on

compliance." *Group Processes & Intergroup Relations* 14, no. 5 (September 2011): 671–680.

141. Zhang, Y. Charles, and Norbert Schwarz. "How and Why 1 Year Differs from 365 Days: A Conversational Logic Analysis of Inferences from the Granularity of Quantitative Expressions." *Journal of Consumer Research* 39, no. 2 (August 2012): 248–259.

142. Smith, Robert W., David Faro, and Katherine A. Burson. "More for the Many: The Influence of Entitativity on Charitable Giving." *Journal of Consumer Research* 39, no. 5 (March 2013): 961–976.

143. Atalay, A. Selin, H. Onur Bodur, and Dina Rasolofoarison. "Shining in the Center: Central Gaze Cascade Effect on Product Choice." *Journal of Consumer Research* 39, no. 4 (December 2012): 848–866.

144. Riener, Gerhard, and Christian Traxler. "Norms, moods, and free lunch: Longitudinal evidence on payments from a Pay-What-You-Want restaurant." *Journal of Socio-Economics* 41, no. 4 (August 2012): 476–483.

145. Brough, Aaron R., and Mathew S. Isaac. "Finding a Home for Products We Love: How Buyer Usage Intent Affects the Pricing of Used Goods." *Journal of Marketing* 76, no. 4 (July 2012): 78–91.

146. Elder, Ryan S., and Aradhna Krishna. "The 'Visual Depiction Effect' in Advertising: Facilitating Embodied Mental Simulation through Product Orientation." *Journal of Consumer Research* 38, no. 6 (April 2012): 988–1003.

147. Brough, Aaron R., and Alexander Chernev. "When Opposites Detract: Categorical Reasoning and Subtractive Valuations of Product Combinations." *Journal of Consumer Research* 39, no. 2 (August 2012): 399–414.

148. Budría, Santiago. "The shadow value of employer-provided training." *Journal of Economic Psychology* 33, no. 3 (June 2012): 494–514.

149. Maxham III, James G., Richard G. Netemeyer, and Donald R. Lichtenstein. "The Retail Value Chain: Linking Employee Perceptions to Employee Performance, Customer Evaluations, and Store Performance." *Marketing Science* 27, no. 2 (March–April 2008): 147–167.

150. Staats, Bradley R., Katherine L. Milkman, and Craig R. Fox. "The team scaling fallacy: Underestimating the declining efficiency of larger teams." *Organizational Behavior & Human Decision Processes* 118, no. 2 (July 2012): 132–142.

151. Blanes i Vidal, Jordi, and Mareike Nossol. "Tournaments Without Prizes: Evidence from Personnel Records." *Management Science* 57, no. 10 (October 2011): 1721–1736.

152. Fesenmaier, Kimm. "Neuroscientists Find That Status Within Groups Can Affect IQ." HealthCanal.com, January 23, 2012. http://www.healthcanal.com/brain-nerves/25686-Neuroscientists-Find-That-Status-within-Groups-Can-Affect.html.

153. Enayati, Amanda. "Workplace Happiness: What's the Secret?" CNN, July 9, 2012. http://articles.cnn.com/2012-07-09/living/living_secret-to-workplace-happiness_1_id-badges-productivity-workplace.

154. Shea, Christopher. "A Creative Buzz." *Wall Street Journal* online, February 22, 2012. http://blogs.wsj.com/ideas-market/2012/02/22/a-creative-buzz/.

155. Tierney, John. "From Cubicles, Cry for Quiet Pierces Office Buzz." *New York Times*, May 19, 2012. http://www.nytimes.com/2012/05/20/science/when-buzz-at-your-cubicle-is-too-loud-for-work.html.

156. Thomas, Manoj, and Claire I. Tsai. "Psychological Distance and Subjective Experience: How Distancing Reduces the Feeling of Difficulty." *Journal of Consumer Research* 39, no. 2 (August 2012): 324–340.

157. "Study suggests disarmingly simple way to better job ethics: Slow down." Academy of Management,

January 1, 2012. http://aom.org/News/Press-Releases/Study-suggests-disarmingly-simple-way-to-better-job-ethics--slow-down%281%29.aspx.

158. Zhong, Chen-Bo. "The Ethical Dangers of Deliberative Decision Making." *Administrative Science Quarterly* 56, no. 1 (March 2011): 1–25.

159. "Trusting Feelings When Predicting Future Events: The Emotional Oracle Effect," *Science Daily*, February 24, 2012. http://www.sciencedaily.com/releases/2012/02/120224140512.htm.

160. Sauer, Stephen J. "Why Bossy Is Better for Rookie Managers." *Harvard Business Review* 90, no. 5 (May 2012): 30.

161. McCombs, Kristin, Bryan Raudenbush, Andrea Bova, and Mark Sappington. "Effects of Peppermint Scent Administration on Cognitive Video Game Performance." *North American Journal of Psychology* 13, no. 3 (2011): 383–390.

162. Burgmer, Pascal, and Birte Englich. "Bullseye! How Power Improves Motor Performance." *Social Psychological and Personality Science* 4, no. 2 (March 2013): 224–232.

163. Jacob, Céline, Nicolas Guéguen, Angélique Martin, and Gaëlle Boulbry. "Retail salespeople's mimicry of customers: Effects on consumer behavior." *Journal of Retailing & Consumer Services* 18, no. 5 (September 2011): 381–388.

164. Converse, Benjamin A., Jane L. Risen, and Travis J. Carter. "Investing in Karma: When Wanting Promotes Helping." *Psychological Science* 23, no. 8 (August 2012): 923–993.

165. "Happiness at Work Insights Emerging, Delivering Happiness at Work." October 18, 2012. http://deliveringhappinessatwork.com/happiness-at-work-insights-emerging/.

acknowledgments

This book is the work of many hands and many minds. I can't possibly list all of my colleagues who have suggested items for the Daily Stat over the years, but their contributions are greatly appreciated. I owe special thanks to Eric Hellweg for introducing the idea of publishing a Daily Stat e-newsletter and to the entire Harvard Business Digital team for nurturing the project in its early days. Thanks also to Tim Sullivan for a thoughtful read of the book manuscript and to Harvard Business Publishing's editorial, design, and production teams for a dazzling finished product.

about the author

Andrew O'Connell is an editor with the Harvard Business Review Group.